2/9/11

HealthSouth
The Wagon to Disaster

To Phyllis and Jennifer

HealthSouth
The Wagon to Disaster

Aaron Beam
with
Chris Warner

Wagon Publishing
Fairhope, AL 36532
© 2009

Printed in the USA
ISBN 10: 0-9796284-8-2
ISBN 13: 978-0-9796284-8-1

Acknowledgment

There are many people I would like to acknowledge in the writing of this book. However, one person's assistance was singular. I must particularly thank Weston Smith for his generous contribution. Chapter nine is about Weston's involvement and chapter ten was written solely by him. In my mind, it is the highlight of the book. Because I left the company in 1997, Weston's input regarding what happened at HealthSouth from 1997 until 2003 was invaluable. Undoubtedly, this book could not have been written without Weston's help. Thank you much, Weston Smith.

Aaron Beam
September 2009

Table of Contents

HealthSouth
The Wagon to Disaster
By Aaron Beam
With Chris Warner

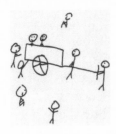

Preface

After losing possessions, serving prison time, and fully coming to terms with what happened, I understand that I have committed a terrible, white-collar crime that hurt many people. Because of a lack of conviction, I will always be remembered as the guy that committed the fraud instead of the co-founder of one of America's most successful health care companies.

Friends and colleagues had encouraged me to write a book, and it was something that I had always strongly considered, as this story is larger than any individual. Corporate fraud is an ongoing, problematic theme in modern American business history. Its greedy pervasiveness—evidenced in the wake of the Worldcom, Tyco, and Enron fiascoes and more recently in the sub-prime mortgage debacle, is threatening the health of our economy and its ability to operate based on public trust.

This book is my opportunity to help the business world understand how and why the fraud at HealthSouth happened, and how it can happen to them if they aren't careful. I am proud to finally tell the truth behind HealthSouth. Since the fraud became public, HealthSouth has paid restitution and rebounded; it is still traded on the New York Stock

Exchange and it remains a viable health care provider at its many locations throughout the United States.

The title of the book has particular meaning among those familiar with HealthSouth, the corporation. In meetings Richard Scrushy often used the motivating mantra, "Pulling the Wagon" to remind everyone of the importance of pulling his or her weight for the HealthSouth "team." Richard had tee shirts and posters printed with a sketch of several stick figures pulling a wagon, and he even had a fancy sculpture of metal stick figures pulling a wagon erected in front of the HealthSouth Birmingham offices. For those of us "Pulling the Wagon," we soon realized it was all for Richard, and in the end he was leading all of us to a sure disaster.

Aaron Beam
January, 2009

Introduction

I was relaxing and watching the evening news at my recently-finished, sprawling retirement home at Beam Acres in Fairhope, Alabama when the announcer said, "We open tonight's broadcast with a breaking story from Birmingham, Alabama. A massive accounting fraud at HealthSouth Corporation has been revealed. Early reports indicate that the fraud has been going on for several years and may exceed $2 billion." I immediately felt as sick as I did helpless. The day I had long feared finally arrived. I thought, "This can't be! It has been so long…"

The next day I read in the Mobile *Press Register* that the United States Attorney for the Northern District of Alabama, Alice Martin, was asking that anyone involved with the fraud come forward. My wife Phyllis tried to tell me not to worry. She was sure I had been gone long enough from the company that I was clear of any wrongdoing. Phyllis knew about the fraud, as I had told her, but I had never really gone into the details. I assured her that I should be worried.

Phyllis and I decided that we would call Jay Johnson, the attorney we hired when we started HealthSouth. Over the years Jay and I had formed a good relationship. He left his law firm about the same time I left HealthSouth to become an in-house counsel for Med-Partners, one of many companies created by HealthSouth CEO Richard Scrushy after the emergence and dominance of HealthSouth. Although I was aware that the Med-Partners relationship did not go well and that Jay had sued Med-Partners and Richard Scrushy.

Jay agreed to meet with Phyllis and me in Montgomery. I was pretty sure Jay would not be the attorney to represent me, but I still wanted his legal insight and hiring recommendations. Jay could also answer an important question: Had the statute of limitations expired? Had I really been gone long enough to be safe from Federal punishment?

Jay was extremely kind and understanding. He knew Richard Scrushy well and understood exactly how I got myself into the trap. Surprisingly, however, Jay had no recommendation for a lawyer. He said the attorneys in Birmingham were being claimed in a rush. He was not even sure if there was suitable counsel in the metro region left to be hired. He suggested I look to the Mobile area for help. He also said that he would look into the question regarding the statute of limitations.

I called Ken Riemer, a lawyer and friend from Mobile, who was an LSU graduate. He and I met at one of the crawfish boils I had at Beam Acres. He recommended Donald Briskman as the best white collar crime lawyer in Mobile. I called Briskman's office and he encouraged me to come see him immediately.

That afternoon Phyllis and I sat across from Donald at his office table. I told him my story. Phyllis was crying and it was all I could do to hold it together. Donald can be intimidating and he was not putting me at ease, but I don't believe anyone could have under the circumstances. Donald gave me some good advice, however. He said, "From this point forward you must tell the truth."

Donald had already spoken to a friend of his, George Martin, a lawyer from the Mobile area who worked in Alice Martin's United States Attorneys office. He assured me that Alice indeed wanted to talk to me. Donald explained that her office was well aware of my role in the fraud and that the FBI was all over the HealthSouth headquarters. He instructed me that it would not pay to attempt to lie my way out of the situation, as the consequences for lying would be severe.

Before Phyllis and I left, Donald set up a meeting with the government for the following week in Birmingham. I asked Donald if he needed a check at this time. He said yes, and that I needed to make it for $100,000. For a second I thought he might be kidding, but I quickly realized it was no joking matter. He explained that this would likely not be the only check of this magnitude I would have to write him. Luckily, Phyllis and I had recently sold our New Orleans condominium and I was able to cover it. As I begrudgingly wrote the check I realized that my life would never be the same.

***

While this story is told primarily from my point of view, it is not really about me; it's undoubtedly about Richard Marin Scrushy, one of the most enigmatic, nefarious, chilling and truly fascinating human beings the State of Alabama has produced and certainly one of the worst CEO's to emerge from the noted ranks of American business. Without Richard Scrushy, there wouldn't be a HealthSouth, much less a book about it.

When I first met Richard Scrushy I had misgivings about working for him. Something about him told me that the things he promised were just too good to be true. Nevertheless, I went to work for him because he had a brilliant business mind. As it turned out, it was his only redeeming quality as a human being.

As brilliant as Richard was in his business dealings, he was equally diabolical, callous and cruel in his justification for attaining success. Unbeknownst to me from the onset was the fact that Richard was an egotist of the highest order, a consummate narcissist, likely a sociopath, and one of the biggest liars and fraudsters to ever lead a Fortune 500 company.

There were many nuances of Richard's personality and character that were revealed to me slowly over the time that we worked together to form and build HealthSouth into one of America's most successful health care companies. For instance, I had no idea Richard could play the piano and sing, or that he had more than a casual interest in becoming a rock or country and western music star. Richard is an extremely complex individual. As long as I knew him, I never knew him to have any real friends, because he was a workaholic and constantly had to be the center of attention, the object of everyone's desire. With Richard, if he was not part of the solution, he was the problem.

As time passed and HealthSouth's success grew exponentially, so did Richard's quirkiness. Strangely, he became less concerned with the company and more focused with his musical aspirations—like his country

12

and western band consisting of former Nashville musicians named "Dallas County Line" or his all-girl glam band called "3rd Faze" that opened for Britney Spears and inked a record deal because he gave the Vice President of *Sony* Records a gift of 250,000 shares of HealthSouth stock. Moreover, Richard even paid for breast augmentation for 3rd Faze's teenage members. Predictably, the wealthier Richard became, his lifestyle became equally more excessive.

It is estimated that over his nineteen-year business career with HealthSouth and his other companies, Richard made nearly $1 billion in compensation. Conservative estimates put the figure closer to $900 million. Richard was not only HealthSouth's CEO and Chairman of the Board—a position that allowed him a more than generous salary, bonus package and stock options, he was also a principal or equity investor in 12 other health care companies, many of which entitled him to receive either additional compensation in the form of a related salary and/or bonus packages and stock options. Richard used this unprecedented wealth—he was a former gas station attendant, day laborer and brick layer—to purchase 11 mansions and homes, nearly 40 automobiles—including a Lamborghini Merciaglo and a bullet-proof BMW, 15 jet airplanes, a seaplane, a Sikorsky helicopter, a 92-foot yacht, countless recreational boats and jet skis, three wives, nine children, vast political and social influence within Birmingham, the State of Alabama and Washington, D.C., as well as a half-hearted attempt at a professional music career.

Money became of little concern to Richard, especially when it was HealthSouth's money--evidenced by the way he built monuments to himself throughout the City of Birmingham, Alabama, where HealthSouth's headquarters were located. Highways, daycare centers, ball fields, libraries, colleges, statues and conference centers all bore his name or likeness; and the city—like HealthSouth's management, employees and stockholders—were in the end all equally fooled by his grand façade built on deception and lies.

When the securities fraud case against Richard surfaced in 2003, he demonstrated his uncanny knack for reinventing himself yet again by becoming a televangelist that catered to the black community in

Birmingham. Richard used his wealth to purchase a small local television station and in an overtly shameless effort to taint the jury pool, he began preaching every morning on his self-produced program titled "Viewpoint," in which he would parade a constant line of seemingly unsuspecting African-American preachers and reverends. Richard also gave generously to their congregations—doling out millions to build churches and meeting facilities within their respective, needy, inner-city communities. The insidiously brash investment paid off—the majority black Federal jury of seven blacks and five whites found Richard Marin Scrushy not guilty on 32 counts ranging from bribery to securities and bank fraud. Tragically, unbeknownst to the black preachers and their faithful followers, Richard Scrushy as HealthSouth CEO had adamantly maintained a well-known "No black hiring rule." It was only after Richard and the company management found itself in jeopardy that he hired HealthSouth's first black employee.

This story is not only the complete, untold story of HealthSouth, it's really the story of the larger tragedy caused by Richard Marin Scrushy--to not only the duped shareholders, but also to the former company employees and the larger Birmingham and Alabama communities. The collective pain and harm done to all of these people will take decades to undo. Furthermore, it is uncertain that they will ever recover from his crimes. All of this was done because of the sickness of one man—and I had the chance to stop him; but unfortunately, I didn't and it has made all the difference.

1

The First Time I met Richard Scrushy

"Brilliant Businessman or Con Artist?"

I worked for Richard Scrushy for less than thirty minutes when I heard him tell a brazen lie.

I went home and told my wife, Phyllis, that I had, "Just interviewed with the biggest con artist or the most brilliant young man I had ever met." Later, I told her either way, I was taking the job, because he (Richard) was "Really, really good at what he did."

In the summer of 1980, I interviewed in Houston, Texas with 30-year-old Richard Marin Scrushy, Vice President of the Shared Services Division for Lifemark, a hospital management company traded on the New York Stock Exchange, for the position of controller.

Until the time I interviewed with Lifemark, I had always worked with smaller companies with much less infrastructure. I felt that at age 37 it was time for me to join ranks with a company in which I could grow.

While working at Johnson Cover Company from 1976-1980, I attended the University of Houston and took the accounting courses necessary to qualify for the CPA exam. I earned my CPA certificate in 1978. One of the qualifications for the job at Lifemark was that the applicant be a certified public accountant.

16

I liked the idea of being able to own stock in the company I worked for, so I was genuinely excited about starting at Lifemark and the bright future it could bring me and my family. The smaller companies I had worked for hadn't done much. I felt it was time to move into the corporate world, as the pay was more competitive. At Lifemark, starting out I made about $30,000 annually, while Richard was likely making twice that.

When I was hired at Lifemark, Richard Scrushy was Vice President of the Respiratory Therapy Company, a department within Lifemark's Shared Services Division. There were three companies in this division—Respiratory Therapy, Physical Therapy, and Pharmacy.

Richard's expertise was in respiratory therapy, so he was the Vice President for the respiratory therapy division. As his controller, or finance person, my responsibilities were budgeting, new business analysis, review of financial results, and assisting operations on financial matters.

Richard's respiratory therapy acumen came from extensive education and work experience in the medical field. In 1971, he was a former gas station attendant looking for direction and a rung on the success ladder. After walking off a bricklaying job site, at the advice of his mother, he enrolled full-time at Wallace State Community College in his rural home town of Selma, Alabama while working full-time at other odd jobs. A year later, he transferred from Wallace, which was known affectionately by locals as "Harvard on the Highway," to Jefferson State Community College in Birmingham and worked nights in a local hospital's respiratory therapy program. Richard married at age 17, with a baby already on the way, and prior to finishing community college, he and his wife were already parenting two children.

Born in 1952 to a nurse and a NCR (National Cash Register) cash register salesman, Richard was not a privileged person. Growing up in Selma, Richard was the quintessential American boy. He went by his middle name, Marin, attended Methodist Church with his family, was a Boy Scout, and played little league baseball. However, as he grew older, his life became more complicated. During his teenage years he was in a band, wore a large, bushy, afro, and it was widely-known that he was an aspiring music star. Friends said that he wanted to be "like Elvis." However, he was more of a hood than anything, as his extra-curricular pursuits caused him to leave the parochial high school program he started in order to finish his secondary studies at Dallas County High. Moreover, he reportedly used to invite guests into his trailer park home where he'd serve them wine and champagne, undoubtedly a laughable foreboding of future escapades.

After he passed the respiratory therapy technician exit exam, Richard enrolled in the respiratory therapy program at the University of Alabama at Birmingham (UAB). After graduation in 1974, he became an instructor in the program he had just completed. Shortly thereafter, he was promoted to program director and spent two and a half years teaching at UAB. During these early years, Richard paid his bills and covered his education costs by working in the evenings as a respiratory therapist at local hospitals.

Richard later left Birmingham to become the director of the respiratory therapy program at Wallace State Community College in Dothan, Alabama. At Wallace State, Richard met and began dating his second wife, one of his students, Karon. A year later, he joined Lifemark.

Lifemark not only owned hospitals, it also managed parts of hospitals it did not own. For instance, Lifemark managed many respiratory departments within non-owned hospitals that wanted to use its better technology, its better-trained personnel and its cost-saving ability. Richard was extremely aggressive in bringing in these contracts, and he was fantastic at it. He was truly a great salesperson; in fact, he carried the Lifemark mantle much better than all of his bosses. Nevertheless, even early on I had misgivings about his tactics.

The first day at work for Lifemark I was like any new employee, enthusiastic. I arrived at 7:30 a.m., thirty minutes early. At 8:00 a.m., Richard called me to his office. He told me that he wanted me to go with him to present a proposal for signing a new contract to his boss. I said sure. We went to his boss's office and Richard introduced us. We sat and Richard said, "Aaron and I stayed up late last night working on these numbers and we think we need to sign this contract."

I was stunned. I hadn't worked with Richard 30 minutes and he'd already told a lie. It wasn't a huge lie, but the brazen way in which he told it made me wonder. Later, as the years went by, I often reflected on this first lie told by Richard. I always wondered if he tested me that first morning on the job—to see if I would go along with him.

Within two years Richard Scrushy was promoted to Vice President of all three companies (respiratory, physical and pharmacy) in the division. I was promoted with him as his financial guy. We contracted with hospitals for a set percentage of the department's revenue. We had about 100 of these contracts in our division. Lifemark assisted with staffing, providing equipment, clinical expertise, as well as ongoing, on-the-job education.

During these early days at Lifemark, Richard recruited Gene Smith from Wisconsin and Anthony Tanner from New York, both respiratory therapists and eventual HealthSouth founders with me and Richard.

One of the first things I learned about Richard Scrushy was that he did not like having a boss. He spent hours every week griping to me about his boss, his family life and his many problems with his ex-wife (he had recently married Karon but had two kids with his first wife). I soon realized that you had to be Richard Scrushy's "boy" and that you could not avoid him—he demanded your attention.

At the time when I worked with Richard at Lifemark he was about 20 to 25 pounds over his ideal weight. He was not overly fat, but I could tell he was sensitive about his weight and his increasing hair loss. Moreover, he smoked, as did four of the top six managers. None of the physical or pharmacy managers smoked, which I found odd, because most of the managers in the field smoked often. Ironically, Lifemark had a number of managers overseeing the provision of cutting-edge respiratory care—and they smoked cigarettes.

19

Richard was not liked by the other Lifemark company heads from physical therapy and pharmacy. He was so competitive with them that he always made them look bad at company meetings, group settings, and presentations.

Richard and I both learned most of what we knew about managing a large organization from Lifemark. The Chairman of the Board (C.O.B.), Bill Mackey, was a former accounting professor at Rice University. Bill was extremely smart and intimidating. He was known to skip chain of command and ask questions about financial statements, and he was the only person I've ever known Richard Scrushy to fear.

Bill Mackey managed by the numbers. Each month within five business days of the month's end we reviewed profit and loss statements, having to explain large variances. Richard Scrushy reported to the executive vice president who reported to the president.

Lifemark's accounting was centrally located. There were strict operational controls over hospitals across the South from Lifemark's Houston headquarters. Everything was centralized. All bills and payrolls were paid and distributed from the corporate headquarters.

Lifemark believed strongly in corporate meetings where the operating unit managers would have to come to Houston or some other central site to receive training and corporate indoctrination. Later, Richard and I followed this same blueprint for HealthSouth.

At the time Richard received an annual bonus and stock options and I remember in 1983 he purchased a used Mercedes Benz and was really proud of it, as status was always important to him. And just as Richard spent much time talking to me about his boss and company politics, each year he complained about the size of his bonus. Money was so important to him. It was painful for me to listen to this, because I was ineligible for a bonus, but Richard was not concerned how I felt.

Richard enjoyed meetings. He loved leading them and they were an important part of his teaching/management style in which he really excelled. He loved being the focus, the show; he was really a sharp, clever guy.

Richard took an American Management Association course "Accounting for non-financial managers" in Chicago. I was blown away at how fast he learned it. It seemed as if he acquired in two weeks what it took me years to comprehend. Richard was not only smart--he was crafty; even when he stumbled.

One of our regional respiratory therapy meetings for Lifemark was held in Memphis. After the meeting Richard took everyone in attendance to a nearby upscale gentleman's club and paid for everyone's drinks—not their entertainment. Richard expensed the drinks in his expense report.

The internal auditors investigated the suspicious name on the credit card bill and discovered that it was a strip joint. They weren't happy, and they demanded a full written explanation of the activity. Richard obliged. He spent several days working on a letter. He explained that in lieu of an evening meal, which was certainly a legitimate expense, he purchased drinks for everyone. He defended this by saying that despite the type of entertainment they enjoyed that evening, that the meeting was a rousing success; he audaciously attributed much of the quarter's success to the team-building and camaraderie that occurred because of the Memphis meeting. The letter worked. As far as I know Richard never again heard from the auditors.

Socially, my wife Phyllis and I did not do a lot with Richard and Karon. Just like at work, Richard always had to be the center of attention; and his conversations were almost always about work, so it was like being at the office when you were with him in what was supposed to be a relaxed social setting. Richard was so into his work that he rarely had any personal time. In fact, he had little down time, from what I recall. Everything was work to Richard; and it transformed him. I do remember a surprise birthday party that his wife Karon gave him. He loved it. As

21

usual, Richard, the cynosure, adored being the focal point, the sought after, the object of everyone's attention.

Nevertheless, on many days I would have to eat with Richard because he considered it business, but you always had to eat where he wanted to eat. He would often say, "Don't you guys want to go to Soup N' Salad to eat lunch today? Why, you'd be a fool not to want to go to Soup N' Salad for lunch!" It was all semantics for Richard, but that's how he was—he had to have his way all the time.

In late 1983 Richard began talking to Lifemark management about free-standing, therapy clinics. There were also merger talks. Shortly thereafter the headline on the front page of the *Wall Street Journal* read: "AMI to purchase Lifemark." The sub headline read: "AMI to close Houston office."

2

My Life Before HealthSouth

"The Apple Falls Near the Tree"

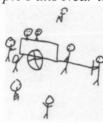

My father grew up in Pleasant Hill, in North Louisiana, 50 miles south of Shreveport. My mother grew up in Texas, Arkansas and Louisiana. Dad met Mother in Shreveport and they were married in 1940. I was born in November, 1943, in Shreveport, the second of five children.

After serving as a cook in the United States Army during World War II, dad returned home and operated a popular eatery in Shreveport known as the J-Hawk Café, the first of many enterprises.

Dad's next venture was named G.I. Novelty, a pinball, jukebox and other coin-operated machines business he started with friends. Their office was next to a restaurant, bar and liquor store in which they all shared an ownership interest. The bar was called K-9, and my dad told me that Hank Williams was a frequent customer. Dad used to also say that no artist had ever been played more on jukeboxes than Hank Williams. In those days "honky-tonk joints," as they were called, played his music almost non-stop.

One of my fondest childhood memories involved cleaning up the K-9 with my older sister, Janice, on Sunday mornings. For a kid it was cool to be inside the bar, as we were not normally allowed in the establishment during working hours. The place, of course, had a distinctive, sour smell the day after a big Saturday night, and our job was to recycle the beer bottles and to generally straighten the place. It was also fun because we often found loose change and paper money under the bar and tables.

After a few years dad started his own juke box/pinball business. He constructed a building and opened a similar operation that he had shared prior with his business partners: a bar, liquor store and restaurant. From this point forward dad was always in business for himself. Over the years dad made a lot of money and spent a lot of money, putting five children through college.

I acquired some of my father's not-so-good habits. He liked to drink and gamble. In the 1950's he won $65,000 rolling dice at the Sands Hotel in Las Vegas. Of course, he never told me about the times he lost, but to win $65,000 in 1950's dollars was quite a haul.

I started the first grade just before my sixth birthday. This was before kindergarten. I performed terribly in elementary school. By the end of the fifth grade, school officials met with my parents and told them that I would likely never finish high school, as I was tested and revealed to read only at the second grade level.

As an adult I realized I probably had an extreme case of Attention-Deficit Disorder (ADD), because I was unable to sit still long enough to learn anything. If I were a child today I would probably have to mainline Ritalin. Admittedly, I still have the attention span of a hummingbird; people often comment that I seem hyper-active.

The meeting with my fifth grade teachers made me angry. I knew I wasn't stupid. After that I made a concerted effort to start learning. I didn't understand why I was performing so poorly in school, but I knew I was capable of making better grades.

The hard work paid off. Also, I was fitted with glasses, which helped tremendously. By junior high school I was making B's and C's and a few D's, but no F's. By high school, it was B's and C's and a few A's, but no F's. I excelled in speech and chemistry, participated on the high school debate team and even won a few contests. I finished my secondary schooling with a C-plus average, just below a B, which wasn't too bad for a guy written off by the system.

I graduated Bossier City High School in 1961 with a class of 230 students. Later, in the fall of that year, I attended LSU in Baton Rouge. At first I wanted to be a chemist, so I majored in chemistry. However, after taking calculus during my first semester I quickly switched to business, wanting to take my father's lead. Like he had, I wanted a business career.

I graduated with a B average from LSU in 1967 with an economics degree. This was during the Vietnam War, and I was at the top of the Army draft list. I instead enlisted in the Navy in 1968. After boot camp I was sent to a Naval Communications Station in Western Australia. My job in the Navy was storekeeper, working in the supply department. I was there for 18 months before receiving orders for duty in Vietnam. I was stationed at a military base in SaDec for six months and then in Saigon for another six months.

Phyllis and I were engaged while I was stationed in Australia. We were married in 1970 between my duty in Australia and Vietnam. I had three months of training in San Diego before heading overseas, and Phyllis and I—newlyweds at the time—were able to spend it together.

Luckily I never saw combat in Vietnam. I did have an M-16 issued to me, and with it I once shot a rat at the SaDec landfill. However, I received no medal for this.

I left the Navy as a second-class petty officer (E-5). After an honorable discharge in 1972 I was hired in Houston by a start-up technology company. I was the fifth person hired and the first non-engineer. They were developing a computer control system for chemical plants, and were one of the first outfits to purchase the Mini Computer (Digital Equipment Company), before personal computers became prevalent. The computer was installed in a control panel to monitor temperatures, pressures and flows inside the plants.

I was hired to be the office manager and the accountant. I did everything non-scientific so that the engineers that started the company could develop the product. I administered the payroll, paid the bills, kept the books, hired office personnel, bought insurance and tended to all things administrative. It was a great first job, as I learned a lot; much of it I would later use to start HealthSouth, where I dealt with therapists, instead of engineers.

The company, Control Automation Technology, or CATCO, was funded by wealthy investors, not formal venture capitalists like those at Citicorp who initially invested in HealthSouth. CATCO did well initially. It sold several of its products to large chemical companies. By 1975, we had over 100 employees. But, the second-generation product we developed turned out to have "bugs" that could not be fixed. In 1976, the company folded and I was looking for a job.

This time I went to work for Johnson Cover in Houston, an extremely low-tech company. Johnson manufactured loose leaf binders, index tabs and folders. It was a family-owned business with 50 employees and about $2,000,000 in annual revenues. The Johnson brothers hired me as a controller to help them diversify and grow the company. During the four years I was there I attended the University of Houston where I took the necessary accounting courses to allow me to sit for the Certified Public Accountant (CPA) exam. I took and passed the examination in 1978. This gave me one of the qualifications I would later need to get the Lifemark job. During this same period, Phyllis earned an education degree from the University of Houston and taught in Houston schools.

3

The Dawn of HealthSouth

"Move to California or Move to Alabama"

One morning in the summer of 1983 our division was summoned to a meeting at the corporate office in Houston. We were told that Lifemark was merging with American Medical International (AMI). The next day the story was front page news in the *Wall Street Journal.* The sub-headline said the corporate office of Lifemark would be closed and the company would be managed out of AMI offices in California. We were told that the AMI people would be coming to Houston in the weeks that followed to interview prospective hires. However, we were all asked to stay until the merger was completed.

The closing was estimated to occur just before year's end, in December 1983. The promise was that every employee that stayed until then would receive a severance package. Nevertheless, we soon learned that few Lifemark employees would be retained by AMI, as the *Wall Street Journal* article said the merger made good business sense because of the corporate overhead that would be eliminated in Houston.

During this limbo period Richard began discussions with Matt Mackowski of Citicorp venture capital of San Francisco. Citicorp was interested in funding a start-up company that might result as a fall-out from the merger.

What Matt discovered and told Citicorp was that Richard had an idea for a company that would operate a national chain of outpatient rehab centers. During the previous 20 years, for-profit hospitals had become big business. Public companies like AMI, Hospital Corporation of America (HCA), National Medical Enterprises (NME), and Lifemark were in great favor with Wall Street. However, concern about rising healthcare costs became an issue, evidenced by a simultaneous dip in stock values.

Richard's timing could not have been better. His strategy was that much of the care delivered within the walls of acute care hospitals could be done in outpatient settings. Hospitals have significant overhead costs because patients often must spend the night to be treated. This requires parking, housekeeping, laundry, food services, security, etc. Also, hospitals are constructed to a much higher building code than most buildings and this significantly increases their costs.

At this time, a patient who was well enough to be discharged but needed therapy was often kept at the hospital a few days longer to receive this final part of their health care. But, if the patient could receive this therapy on an outpatient basis after being discharged, one could see the obvious cost-savings inherent with such a switch.

Another part of Richard's strategy was that he knew from working in hospitals that patients would prefer to leave the hospital as soon as possible after surgery. This meant that they would certainly rather enter a facility away from the hospital to receive additional necessary treatment. Parking would be easier and they would not have to remain in a building full of sick people. The environment of the outpatient facility would be far superior.

Richard also knew that even the therapists would rather work in an outpatient setting rather than in the hospital. In the hospital the doctors and nurses are the big dogs—not the therapists. Through HealthSouth we could offer a facility where the therapists and their expertise would be most important. During the 1980's physical therapists were in short supply but we felt we could hire the best of them away from the hospitals.

To assist in getting patients in our centers Richard believed we should allow doctors to invest in them. Doctors would be allowed to invest in HealthSouth's individual centers, not the corporation itself, but the separate operating units. However, we were always sure to retain at least 51% ownership in each unit. This was for control and accounting reasons because we could consolidate the entire operating numbers as ours if we controlled 51%. It was also helpful to have the doctors' money to help grow the company without giving up ownership to the venture capitalists. In those days doctor-invested health care providers were not uncommon. Many of the publicly-held hospital companies began as hospitals owned by doctors. As we began selling partnerships to doctors we found that many of them wanted to invest because they had missed the boat during the previous boom of publicly-traded hospitals. Also, providing ownership options for doctors also helped referrals.

It is important to understand that this outpatient approach to healthcare was extremely cutting-edge. Outpatient surgery and diagnostic centers were just beginning to appear.

There was another important reason we felt this was a strong business model. Medicare had recently approved another healthcare provider, the Comprehensive Outpatient Rehabilitation Facility, or CORF. Prior to this provider, Medicare would not pay for many therapy procedures unless they were done in a hospital. Private insurance, in many cases, was handled the same way. Therefore, the CORF opened the door for reimbursement of such procedures like respiratory, occupational, speech and physical therapy. With America's growing aging population, this was a huge selling point for HealthSouth.

During the merger Richard began telling Gene Smith, Tony Tanner and me about his idea for his new rehabilitation company that would provide high-quality, low-cost health care. Initially, I was not eager to sign up and jump on board. While I had seen Richard achieve great success at Lifemark, working for him was not that much fun. I also was not keen on the idea of working for a small start-up company again. As stated, my first job after college and the United States Navy was with a start-up and it only lasted four years before it failed.

I also had doubts Richard could acquire the financing to start the company. He told me he was talking to the Citicorp venture capitalists and he asked that I have dinner with him and Matt Mackowski. Richard was at his best during the meeting and I saw Matt totally buying into the concept.

Meanwhile, AMI flew Phyllis and me to California to interview for a job with the merged companies. I was offered a controller position for the mobile cat scanning company. The money was more than my job at Lifemark paid, but the job required that we move to California.

By this time Richard had a letter from Citicorp saying they would invest $1,000,000 in his new company. I was impressed because at this juncture Richard had not yet even put together a formal business plan replete with financial projections. He got the letter of intent based solely on his salesmanship.

Richard proposed to Gene, Tony and me that we each put in $5,000 for 100,000 shares in the new company (5 cents per share). He would put in $25,000 for 500,000 shares. Citicorp, on the other hand, would put in $1,000,000 for 1,000,000 shares. On paper, our 100,000 shares were immediately worth $100,000 based on the price Citicorp was willing to pay for theirs.

The plan was that the company would be located in Birmingham, Alabama, and we would begin business in January, 1984. Phyllis and I had a decision to make: move to California away from family and friends and live in a matchbox-sized home or follow Richard to Birmingham. It was not an easy decision. Gene and Tony had already agreed to the deal and were working with Richard on plans for the new company. Phyllis and I made a trip to Birmingham at Richard's request. As we drove into the Fairfield area we saw the unsightly steel works off Interstate 20 and we came really close to turning around. My image of Birmingham prior to the trip was not good, and this realization only made it worse.

However, after a real estate agent showed us houses in the posh Homewood, Mountain Brook, and the Vestavia Hills districts, we quickly warmed to the place.

Richard sweetened the deal for me by offering a salary of $50,000, which was considerably more than what I had made at Lifemark. Matt Mackowski had only agreed to a $60,000 salary for Richard, which was actually a salary cut for him, so we decided after that to go ahead and make the move to Birmingham.

In the last few weeks in Houston while we were waiting for the merger to be completed we began working on a formal business plan for HealthSouth.

4

Raising Venture Capital

"Richard Warned About Insider Dealing"

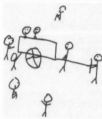

After Richard, Tony, and Gene agreed how the centers would be staffed, how the building would be constructed, and what equipment would be needed, I began creating the financial model. Tony assisted me over my dining room table. Richard advised me as to salaries and other primary fixed costs. We developed a model replete with projected revenues, for a typical center. Citicorp would only fund the $1,000,000 after we had completed a formal 5-year business plan, relocated to Birmingham, and actually opened a corporate office.

Our desire was to become a publicly-traded company like Lifemark. To do this we knew we had to project really great numbers. The first draft of the business plan had us becoming a $100,000,000 company (annual revenues) by the end of the first five years.

At this time the four of us began to fantasize about becoming millionaires. I remember Tony and I laughed about the notion of wealth—it all seemed surreal, but we believed it could happen.

The reality is that you don't become a public company unless you delineate these kinds of numbers. We had to project that big things were coming, or the venture capitalists wouldn't want anything to do with us.

While, in time, HealthSouth would own rehabilitation hospitals, acute care hospitals, surgery and diagnostic centers, the initial business strategy was to be just a pure-play outpatient rehab center company.

I moved to Birmingham in January 1984 and shared an apartment with Tony Tanner. Phyllis stayed in Houston to sell our home in the Montrose area of town. Richard rented a small two-room office in order to establish our corporate headquarters. We operated off of the money we had invested because Citicorp had not yet provided their share, based on their strict stipulations. Because of this, things were really tight. I recall going to the furniture store to purchase our first set of office furniture, which consisted of a couple of cheap folding metal tables and chairs and a single filing cabinet. In retrospect, those were scary times. I remember asking myself, "What if Citicorp pulls out for some reason?" It would have been terrible. The small amount of money we had would have never been able to get the company off the ground.

The office space was so limited and meagerly furnished that we just did most of the work out of our apartment. We kept refining the business plan and setting up shop. We opened a bank account with AmSouth Bank, and interviewed security lawyers, and accounting firms.

We wanted to do everything correctly so that we could go public when the time came, without having to wait. We selected J. Brooke Johnson of Haskell-Slaughter & Young as our security attorney. He was recommended to Richard by Larry House. Also, Peat, Marwick & Mitchell became our Big Eight accounting firm.

Richard convinced several of the hospitals we had contracted with at Lifemark to cancel their contract with AMI and do business with us. The revenues from these contracts, managed by Gene Smith, allowed us to make a profit our first month in business. However, there was a problem. AMI was not at all happy about us taking away business they purchased via the merger with Lifemark. We soon received a letter threatening legal action if we did not return the contracts to AMI. We quickly did. It made no sense to spend our meager funds in a lawsuit or explain to potential investors how we had already gotten ourselves into a legal dispute.

Richard began meeting with local doctors about opening a center in Birmingham. He also was interviewing potential employees who could put together the doctor partnerships. At the same time we were working hard to partner with doctors in Little Rock, Arkansas to open our first center.

We soon closed on the Citicorp deal and had use of our $1,000,000. That was a huge relief. This gave us the funds necessary to begin building out the center in Little Rock. We chose to make leasehold improvements in an existing building to preserve capital. We moved our corporate office near Highway 280 and Highway 459 in a Birmingham Realty office building. We were a tenant in that location until we built our own building just down the highway in 1996.

The $1,000,000 was going fast and we were already talking to other venture capitalists about our second round of financing. Citicorp did a great job of putting us in touch with such respected firms as First Century Partners, Smith Barney, William Blair Venture Partners, and Allstate Insurance. This time we raised six million dollars at a price of $2.50 per share.

These firms were able to get us invited to speak at investor conferences held by other investment banking firms. Our first presentation was in San Francisco at the Robertson, Colman & Stephens Conference. Robertson Stephens was a San Francisco-based boutique investment bank focused primarily on health care and technology companies. I attended the conference with Richard. Other companies like Hospital Corporation of America and National Medical Enterprise were also there. It was exciting. We were one of a few non-public companies making a presentation. These types of conferences were attended by institutional investors like mutual funds, large banks, pension funds, and a few wealthy individuals. We spoke to investors who we hoped to one day own our stock as a publicly traded company. The presentation was the first of hundreds we made during my thirteen years at HealthSouth.

Richard and I were moving into uncharted waters. Many of the things we had to do to get the company started we had never done. It was interesting and we had to learn fast. The people attending these conferences were seasoned and sophisticated. In fact, Richard and I sat in on many presentations so as to learn the ropes on how to present. Each presentation was 30 minutes followed by a "breakout" session with individuals who wanted to ask more questions. Richard made the 30-minute presentation and I helped him answer questions in the breakout. Richard really excelled at these conferences and soon we were a popular invite to other conferences. The room always filled when Richard spoke.

Richard and I had never raised venture capital, written a business plan, presented at investor conferences, or mingled with powerful fund managers. Often in life the fear of the unknown is the worst. But, once you get into the game and take a few hits you realize it isn't so bad. We quickly realized after listening to other company presentations that we had as good a story as anyone--and more importantly--could probably tell it better than most.

Completing our second round of venture capital financing was much more involved than getting the first million from Citicorp. We visited with firms in Birmingham and other cities across the country. In all we met with approximately 30 different venture capital firms. Many did not warm to our plan. One venture capitalist company visited with us in our offices and a few days later called and said he was not interested.

We later learned through Citicorp that the uninterested venture capitalist left our office and went straight to a local hospital. The administrator reportedly told him that we offered "nothing new to healthcare." He assured the venture capitalist that everything we planned to do could be done in a hospital—and better. In the beginning, the local hospital was our competitor. We had to get their customers. While we received many rejections from venture capitalists, Matt Mackowski said our success rate was well above average. When we closed the deal for over $6 million the *Birmingham News* said it was the largest venture capital deal ever closed in the City of Birmingham.

Our plan was to be an outpatient company only. However, we discovered as we were putting our doctor partnership together in various states that many cities needed a rehabilitation hospital. There were only 55 in the United States at the time, in 1984. Lakeshore in Birmingham was one of those hospitals.

A rehabilitation hospital, as its name suggests, specializes in rehabilitative care. There are no surgery rooms, or intensive care center units in a rehab hospital. The patients probably have been hurt, or had major surgery, but are not sick. Many are transferred to a rehab hospital after a stay in an acute care facility. Such patients could be recovering from a car accident, work accident, a broken hip, etc. These types of patients need intense physical and occupational therapy. They are still too injured to receive outpatient care.

Communities actually called us to see if we could build them rehab hospitals. Richard, always the visionary, believed we could do it. It scared the shit out of me. It cost us about $300,000-$400,000 to build and equip an outpatient center. On the other hand, it required about $5 million to build a rehab hospital. While I did have hospital experience from Lifemark, I had never really worked on that side of the house, so to speak. I saw this as a huge leap. Richard did not.

Once again, Richard's plan was cutting-edge. There was an 88-bed skilled nursing facility (SNF) for sale in Florence, South Carolina. The facility had recently been built but never opened because the investment group building it ran out of money. Richard and Tony researched what medical procedures could be provided in a SNF. The answer was much of what is done in a rehab hospital can be done in an SNF. Also, Medicare and private insurance would pay. We acquired the facility for much less than $5 million, equipped it and had our first in-patient facility. This was big. A typical out-patient facility could generate $1-2 million annually in revenue. But an in-patient facility could generate five times that much, or $10 million annually, because patients receive daily therapy, drugs, nursing care and of course, room and board.

It is necessary to explain how important Tony Tanner was during these early days. Tony had a doctorate and was a gifted writer. Furthermore, he worked like a horse. A new company has an insatiable need for written documentation, but this is especially more so for a healthcare company. You cannot receive any legal certification from a health care provider without detailed written policies and procedures. Tony churned out paperwork like magic. I still wonder how he was able to do what he did. When we bought the SNF Richard asked Tony if he could write a procedure manual for such a facility. Tony never blinked an eye. He just started writing. Tony not only wrote all of our medical documentations, he wrote our corporate employee handbooks, policy and procedures and of course he helped write our business plans. While I have talked much about what Richard did, Tony was the ever-so-important man behind the scenes.

Richard had one idea that did not fly. He suggested to Gene, Tony, and I that we form a leasing company that would lease HealthSouth its major assets. He said this would help HealthSouth because it would preserve capital and it would obviously benefit us because of the income and personal tax benefits (depreciation and tax credits). When we asked our lawyer J. Brooke Johnston to draw up the leasing partnership he said, "Wait, you do not want to do this." While it seemed to make sense he pointed out that potential investors would view this as insider dealing. He assured us it would raise all kinds of red flags once we began our public offerings. Richard reluctantly took Johnston's advice. More than anything, Richard never liked being told he could not do something, and in the years to come, despite the warning, Richard probably set a world record in corporate self-dealing.

5

Going Public

"You can Capitalize Those Start-up Costs"

Richard always liked first-of-the-day meetings. One morning in 1985 Richard was the first one in the office. He arrived early to sketch the now-infamous wagon, and its six accompanying stick figure workers pulling and pushing it along. Richard did not make it clear that morning about who he was unhappy with; but, he made it clear with his stick-figure drawings--some of us were not doing our jobs to his satisfaction. He was not specific about what it was we were doing the wrong way; he just said that we were not completely "out front" pulling the wagon, like he felt we should have been, for the HealthSouth "team." Richard purposefully displayed the stick-figure drawing in the office for many following weeks. "Pulling the Wagon" became the de facto company motto and a reproduction of the drawing was framed and hung in every company facility. Tee shirts emblazoned with the drawing were produced and given to the workers. Richard even commissioned an artist to create a life-sized metal sculpture of the stick figures pulling the wagon for the entrance to the HealthSouth headquarters. Everyone at HealthSouth was aware that the boss wanted us to "Pull the Wagon." The mantra was omnipresent.

In 1985 we changed the name of the company from its original name, Amcare, to HealthSouth. Richard felt and I agreed that Amcare sounded too much like many other healthcare companies, and the name was being used in other parts of the United States. Richard wanted something that was unique and stood out among the healthcare field. Also, we knew if we were going to change the name we needed to do so before the company got too big. Richard chose "HealthSouth," as the new name. Amcare was history.

Shortly thereafter, I remember the venture capitalists said that they weren't too keen on the name. Most of them were from the North, so it was understandable. So, I countered with the idea of calling the company, "Dixie Rehab." They replied, "Okay, we'll take HealthSouth."

By the end of 1985 investment bankers began calling on us about a public offering at some point in the future. The likely question was, "When do you 'go' public?" The simple answer is that you can be a publicly owned company at any point, even your first day of business. But with no history of sales and profitable operations the stock will probably trade on the pink sheets at pennies a share. You would be, in effect, "public", but you would be unable to raise serious money with which to grow the company.

We realized we had something when the investment bankers started calling. We were excited. Our growth projections were good, but profitability was improbable, until late 1987 or early 1988. To get there we would have to raise more venture capital, diluting our ownership and not getting us public.

Financially these were tricky times. We were finding a great demand for our rehab centers. We could grow as fast as the money held out, but we were going through it fast. We needed to be profitable to tap the public market. Venture capitalists do not want to pay public prices. There was still the possibility that we could run out of money and have to sell the entire company at an extremely low price. Time was another factor that came into play. The market for companies to become public comes and goes. The market was good at that time, but of course you did not know how long it would last. For example, if you were to try and take a company public today, in 2009, with the current investment climate at a severe low point, it would be almost impossible. Therefore, it was important to act when we did because the window opens and closes.

One of the investment bankers courting us was Drexel Burnham Lambert. While discussing our projected numbers the banker asked Richard and me how we were accounting for start-up costs. I said that we were expensing them. The banker looked at Richard, with a mischievous look, and said, "I bet you can capitalize these costs and reach profitability in a much shorter time." Richard sneered at me and demanded to know why I was not doing this. He said I was "holding the company back" and would certainly not have "the accounting tail wag the company dog."

The accounting theory is that money spent on a business before it begins operations (has revenues), are considered startup costs. These costs can be put on the balance sheet as intangible assets. These assets will benefit future periods of operations and should be written off in the future. The popular treatment was amortization over 60 months after operations begin. We decided to capitalize many activities. We capitalized the salaries of the people who located new sites for us and formed our doctor partnership, as well as a portion of Richard's salary and mine. All employee salary costs at the centers prior to opening were classified as intangible assets. Utilities, rent and every expense at the centers prior to opening were put on the balance sheet. Our outside auditing firm agreed that this was an acceptable accounting practice. We restated our previously published financial statements and reformulated our projections for the coming years. The banker was correct. We forecasted profits in late 1986, instead of 1987.

The stage was set. Most of the bankers said we could go public once we were showing a profit and we believed we could stay profitable. Nevertheless, they warned that a return to losses would be a killer for the stock price.

Richard understood enough about accounting from his Lifemark training to realize that estimating is a big part of it. Richard was certainly familiar with the generalities of the useful life of assets, collectability of revenues and start up costs. Furthermore, accounting for health care revenues is especially judgmental. Bad debts are extremely high in healthcare. People just do not budget for major injury or sickness.

Insurance companies usually do not pay full charges and Medicare has its own payment system. Companies such as HealthSouth must estimate how much they will eventually collect from these various payers. This opens up much room for earnings management.

HealthSouth as a public company would always be judged with suspicion because of these accounting estimates. Some people contend that there was outright fraud almost from the beginning. It is difficult to determine exactly when extremely aggressive accounting estimates turned into pure fraud. Certainly the quality of our numbers declined over time.

Accounting issues aside, HealthSouth was going public. Richard and I began interviewing investment bankers, who are a really competitive lot. They really went after new business. We had meetings with Hambrecht & Quist, Smith Barney, Montgomery Securities, Robertson, Colman & Stephens, Drexel Burnham Lambert, and Alex Brown & Sons. They all made great presentations and assured us they would best support our stock once it began trading. A section of their proposal always had a list of where their firm stood compared to their competitors. Somehow they were always ranked first in the area they said was most important.

In the summer of 1986 we decided that Robertson Colman & Stephens, Drexel Burnham Lambert and Alex Brown & Sons would be our bankers. Robertson was made the lead banker, which is important, because the lead banker runs the show, so to speak. The other bankers, to a degree, are just along for the ride. The lead banker would rather do the deal alone. However, it is best to have a team effort and to some degree pit the bankers against each other.

The going public process begins with the lead banker putting together a schedule. A registration statement (Form S-1) must be written and filed with the SEC for their review. The schedule includes the registration statement and the city stops in the "road show" that followed.

The drafting of the S-1 was one of my most interesting business experiences. A kick-off meeting was held in Atlanta, Georgia at a financial printer's offices. Attending this meeting were representatives from HealthSouth, the three investment banking firms, HealthSouth lawyers, and lawyers representing the investment bankers. Richard, myself, Tony Tanner and Bill Owens represented HealthSouth. Our attorney was J. Brooke Johnston. Each investment bank had at least two or three representatives present during the writing. Once the meeting began the plan was not to leave Atlanta until the document was done and filed with the Securities and Exchange Commission.

The first day lasted about 18 hours. It was grueling. We were creating something that was basically a legal document. The company wanted it to be a sales document, but the attorneys were careful and restricted what we could say. It was truly a product by committee. Everyone in the room contributed. The most difficult part was the beginning, where we had to write about "the company." The first paragraph took over four hours to write.

HealthSouth wanted to say things in the document like "We are a leader in the medical rehabilitation business." The attorneys would counter with, "How do you know you are a leader? What is medical rehabilitation?" Every word and sentence was scrutinized to death. After four hours and only one completed paragraph, I felt we might never finish. But, the process moved along after we became familiarized with how the lawyers liked to word things. At times, tempers flared and it seemed hopeless, but we soon realized that this was the nature of the beast we were wrestling. Our meals were all brought to us and served in the work room. No real breaks were taken. Anyone could take a break but the writing never stopped as long as there were people in the room still working. After three complete days—72 continuous hours—the document was completed and filed with the SEC on September 12, 1986.

Many thousands of copies of the S-1, or Prospectus, were printed and distributed to all offices of the involved investment banking firms. We agreed on the road show schedule put together by the bankers. It slated us for New York, Boston, Minneapolis, San Francisco and London. We began the trek by flying to the offices of Robertson, Colman & Stephens in San Francisco. The first presentation was really just a dress rehearsal for the sales staff. Normally CEO's making their first presentation on a road show need much critiquing and encouraging input to really polish their "act." Richard was an exception. Nevertheless, since it was his first rodeo, he took their constructive comments well. But, after the rehearsal you could plainly see Richard was ready for the road.

In each city we made a breakfast and lunch presentation. Everything was accommodated by the bankers—our flights, ground transportation, hotels and the actual meetings. It was their job to get the buyers to the show. Their salesmen of course had been talking up the company to their clients before our arrival. It was much like the investor conferences we had presented to before, except this time we were the only company making a presentation. The meal was served and then we spoke. During the meal Richard and I sat at separate tables and would take questions from the potential buyers. Firms such as Fidelity, Vanguard, T. Rowe Price, Janus Capital, etc. attended these "dog and pony" shows.

After each meeting as we were traveling to our next city the bankers would tell us what stock orders they'd received after our presentation. We were offering 2,000,000 shares, initially, and there was no real commitment for the firms to actually purchase the number of shares they pledged to purchase. It was really more of a simple show of interest, and the positive buyers were listed in what was called, "The Book," kept by the investment bankers.

There is one other important person in this process that I have not talked about—the stock analyst. Every investment banking firm has an analyst who researches companies and writes reports on them, resulting in a strong buy, buy, hold or sell recommendation. It is against SEC regulations for the bankers to publish a report while a company is in registration—i.e. conducting offerings. However, they are free to talk to potential buyers about the company.

In theory there is a "Chinese Wall" between the analyst and the rest of the banking firm. He is not supposed to be a mouthpiece for the bankers.

In theory the analyst can put out a sell on a client's stock based on anything he thinks is justifiable. Anyone who has really worked with investment bankers probably finds this relationship a little strange. Each of our three bankers assured us their analyst would write about us as soon as the law permitted. We hoped it would be good.

Some analysts on Wall Street are respected and others not so much. Each firm always claims it has the best analyst. This entire portion of our work bringing the company public was entirely interesting to me, as it was a different world that had its own particular rules.

In the beginning the road show was going good, but not great. Richard was wowing the crowds but the stock orders were not coming in big like we needed. The rule-of-thumb is that you need a full book times two. In other words, if we were offering 2,000,000 shares, we needed 4,000,000 in orders. Approaching the end of the road show we had the book times one, but not the book times two, with our last two shows being London and New York, respectively. The last one in New York was considered "the big one."

In London the investment bankers sent a new young man to work with us. He did not know Richard, and he had never been around him. At the end of the day the other brokers and Richard and I went to dinner. After the waiter took our orders, the new banker looked at Richard and said, "Good job today, but your presentation needs a lot of work."

Before anyone could say anything, I glanced at the other two bankers that were more familiar with Richard. Our looks could have been translated into, "Quick—where can we hide?" We knew Richard was going to go berserk, and he did. He called the young man a "fool," a "moron" and a long list of curse words while he twitched uncontrollably and became beet red. It was truly scary the way he retaliated; so much so, that it was difficult to eat our meal.

After we left the investment bankers for the night, Richard was compelled to tell me again what an idiot the fellow who challenged him was. The next day we were told by the banking firm that the young man would not be on the team for the rest of the road show. Richard beat that kid up so bad, I am not sure if he ever recovered.

We flew to New York for the final lunch meeting. Before this meeting we heard that Fidelity had placed an extremely large stock order. This was great news. Fidelity is huge and you really need someone like them in your deal, as they are a financial bell cow. As a result, Richard was really pumped. New York was the biggest stage he had seen. The room was packed and there truly was excitement in the air. At the end of his presentation he received a standing ovation. Right after the ovation, one of the fund managers pulled me aside and said he had never seen anything like it. He commented that people rarely applaud at such events and that they absolutely never stood and clapped.

When Richard and I were in New York, each morning at daybreak we ran in Central Park. I had been a runner most of my life, as it really helped me stay focused. At Lifemark I ran the Tenneco Marathon after training six months. My time for the 26-mile race was three hours and 50 minutes. I was 40, and proud of the time. Because of this experience, Richard always struggled to keep pace with me when we ran, since he was not on my level. Of course, I could tell this bothered him, as he was so competitive.

We left New York feeling good. The prospectus had the price of the stock between $8 and $10 a share. We were told the book was just over 2,000,000 shares. The banker said that to be sure we got the deal done we should lower the price to $6.50. Richard felt that they might be negotiating us down so their job would be easier in the after market once they started trading the next day. Richard even threatened to kill the deal he was so upset. But, he was bluffing. It was all a negotiation act. In the end, Richard gave in, and the next day, September 24, 1986, the stock began trading in the "over the counter market."

During the road show one of the investment bankers told me that we would never have gone public without Richard's great salesmanship. He attributed this to the fact that our last complete year at HealthSouth was only $5 million in total revenues. That year was not profitable. Moreover, we had no record of delivering profits, so it was a bigger investment risk. Yes, we were a young company; yes, Richard was great; but Wall Street wants a longer history of good numbers. This is why we almost didn't go public—but Richard pulled us through. I also remember the investment banker saying that in the future, Richard's ability to promote the company would eventually fade. He said, "The market will only pay attention to the numbers you deliver."

***

During the company's early years we still had much fun despite the long hours we worked. One year, the company signed up for a local softball league. This was classic slow-pitch softball, where your middle-aged team dressed in sweats and tee shirts shows up looking more like drinking buddies than ball players.

The HealthSouth team, under Richard's tutelage, looked different. We showed up with matching crimson jerseys emblazoned with HEALTHSOUTH, white pants and crimson leggings. We looked more suited for a photo shoot at Sears than for a local softball league. We really stood out.

In addition to being our starting pitcher, Richard set the positions and batting lineups. He also offered batting instruction to everyone at practice. In our first game, we were beaten by a score that was more becoming of a homecoming football game. In the subsequent three games we were equally unimpressive. Even with our sparkling uniforms, we were still the league's cellar dweller. Had there been a ten-run rule, we would have had much more time to drink beer after the games. Fed up with losing, Richard decided it was time for a change. He found a couple of former Alabama football players and enlisted their services. Richard offered these ringers money for playing with us--$100 for every home run hit. I remember vividly Richard coming to me and asking for "two or three HealthSouth checks" to pay these Alabama football players. As it turned out, they agreed to the pay, but they refused to wear what they felt were ridiculous white pants and leggings. They played and hit a few lucrative homers. We won a few games. King Richard was happy.

6

We Are All Millionaires

"$30,000 Worth of Neck Ties"

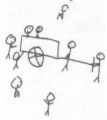

The first few days of trading were extremely exciting. I must have called different brokers 20 times each day to see how the stock was doing. Before long the stock was $10 a share and it was easy to do the math...(100,000 shares x $10 = $1,000,000). The $5,000 I paid for my 100,000 shares in 1984 was now worth $1,000,000! This was pretty heady stuff. Richard, with his 500,000 shares was also doing well. It was the American Dream come true for all of us.

We signed a lock-up agreement not to sell any stock for several months. The bankers asked for this to keep pressure off the stock just after trading began. None of the founders were wealthy when we started the company. We all wanted to sell a little stock so we could begin owning things we previously could not afford. The sale of stock by insiders is always tricky. It is a real Catch 22. On one hand we are telling the public they should buy our stock, but on the other hand we are selling. In the end, however, most investors understand. They realized, as my father used to say, that "You need a little walking around money."

Once the lock-up agreement period was completed, we all sold some of our stock. I think I sold 10,000 shares. I never had $100,000 in cash before. I never even came close to having that kind of money. In fact, I am sure I had never had $10,000 in cash before. This kind of money can change your life.

One Saturday, Phyllis and I had been working in our yard. We worked up quite an appetite and I left to get us burgers. On the way home, I drove by the Mercedes-Benz dealership. It caught my eye. I said to myself, "What the hell." So, I came home that day with not only burgers—but also a new Mercedes Benz. I paid for it with a check. It was not a big Mercedes, but it was still a Mercedes. That was much fun for a guy who had a monthly car payment his entire adult life. Richard's life also soon began to change.

Richard loved nice things, and as his wealth quickly accumulated as a result of his business success, so did his playthings. Richard loved fast cars and airplanes. At one time he had nearly forty automobiles, including a $250,000 Lamborghini and ten homes, including a $10 million, 11,000 square-foot Palm Beach, Florida mansion. When he bought the Lamborghini he insisted on taking me for a ride to show it off. I reluctantly obliged—a decision I later regretted. Richard quickly took the car to outrageous speeds on U.S. Highway 280 in Birmingham. I recall being scared to death as Richard raced the vehicle past 130 miles per hour. I was petrified that we would crash and die.

Richard's love for cars was perhaps eclipsed only by his love of planes. In all, HealthSouth owned ten airplanes, and Richard learned to fly every one of them. In the fleet were two Gulfstream Jets, valued at $25 million apiece, and several smaller, less-expensive jets. I spoke to Ray Ledbetter, the former HealthSouth chief pilot for many years who taught Richard how to fly. Ray said that Richard was an excellent flight student and that he learned to fly airplanes faster than anyone he ever taught. He said that Richard retained 95 percent of the information he presented in each lesson, and learned in a week what took a typical student three months to learn. He said Richard was an excellent pilot, except for the fact that he taxied too quickly on the runway, which was expected given Richard's penchant for speed. Ray told me that after I left the company he and Richard became distant when Richard forced the pilots to stay in roach motels and would not reimburse them for their meals and lodging expenses. Eventually Ray was forced out of his position when

Richard alleged that he took a kickback related to the sale of an airplane. Ray denied taking the bribe.

One of the other extravagant toys Richard enjoyed was his first yacht, a vessel he named the *Kaybee*. Richard was extremely proud of it, and after a particularly grueling stretch of work with HealthSouth, Richard told me to get the finance guys together for a fishing trip.

The boat was moored at a marina in Orange Beach, Alabama, which ironically was later purchased by Richard when his personal wealth reached its zenith. The trip was intended to reward everyone for their hard work, so we were all excited about it. Weston Smith and I rode to the beach in Richard's customized van and all the while we were entertained by Richard pointing out the vehicle's many gaudy features and amenities. Unfortunately for us, the van was outfitted with stereo speakers that were better suited for a rock concert—and Richard pushed them to their limit during the four-hour ride to Lower Alabama, blaring his band's hideous country music CD. When we got to the marina and stepped on to the boat our relieved ears were still ringing. However, we soon realized that the trip would be far from relaxing.

Richard yelled at everyone to "take their God-damned shoes off" because we were getting grass clippings on his brand new deck. After boarding we left the dock and cruised toward the Intracoastal Waterway and the pass at Perdido Point, which opens to the Gulf of Mexico. What happened next was riveting. Upon making the bend from the marina canal into the Intracoastal, the boat was buffeted by strong winds and spun wildly in the opposite direction while we all clung to whatever we could for dear life. Richard, our fearless captain, cursed loudly that the people at the Marina should have warned us about the strong winds. We eventually made it to the pass that opened to the gulf.

As we churned through the pass toward the Gulf of Mexico's open waters I couldn't help feeling like Gilligan in the storm. The yacht again bucked wildly amongst the spray of the angry gulf. Richard wisely decided things were too rough and he quickly reversed our path and returned to the protection of the Intracoastal Canal. However, once we were safely inside the canal Richard failed to reduce our speed. This created an enormous wake on both sides of the waterway. We watched with great interest as an angry coastal resident ran to the end of his pier to secure his boats from the threatening wake. Within a minute the irate man was on his radio yelling for the "Son of a bitch on the Kaybee to slow his ass down!"

We returned to the marina, tails between our legs, all the while having to listen to Richard rant about everyone else's incompetence. After several painstaking hours of sitting in the marina waiting for the weather to clear, Richard decided it was time to make another run at the gulf. This time, Richard decided we would make a run at the gulf from Dolphin Pass, which is farther down the Intracoastal Waterway. The weather had improved, and as a result the mood on the boat was more relaxed. It appeared that we might get to fish after all. Then, suddenly, the boat dragged to an abrupt stop. Richard ran us on to a sand bar! Dan Revere, one of the guys with us, had drank several beers and been quiet the entire afternoon. Richard immediately blamed Dan for not seeing the sand bar and warning us. A while later we finally broke free, but realized that we had bent the props, as the boat only chugged along on the limp back to the marina. Richard of course, ranted, "If only Dan had done his job!" The entire fiasco was a foreshadowing of what was to come, as HealthSouth would encounter many more sandbars, and the captain's reaction was always the same.

Richard obviously had a large ego, but now with serious wealth it was like pouring gasoline on an open fire. Richard was quickly becoming a darling of Wall Street. In October 1987 the stock was trading at $16, up from $6.50 just a year prior. Other health care companies were asking Richard to join their board of directors. For these positions he received a salary and company stock options. Also, the venture capitalists that had backed HealthSouth were bringing investment deals to Richard. Most often, these deals were offered at ground floor company prices—like one or two dollars per share. Richard took full advantage of these emerging situations and profited greatly.

In future years Richard took the lead in funding new companies like Capstone Capital & Medpartners, at an even bigger bargain price of just pennies per share. Simultaneously, Richard was asking the HealthSouth Board of Directors for larger and larger salary increases, annual bonuses and generous stock options. In my estimation, with all of this compensation, Richard was worth over $100,000,000 by the early 1990's. But, he became greedy. Even with all of this wealth, he still wanted more. He was never satisfied.

September 1989 was a significant month for HealthSouth. Our stock moved to the New York Stock Exchange (NYSE) and we purchased South Highlands Hospital in Birmingham, Alabama.

The purchase of South Highlands was important for two reasons: It was an acute care facility and respected doctors Larry Lemak and James Andrews practiced out of this hospital. Nonetheless, Wall Street analysts were confused by this acquisition. We had always said that we could do things better and be more cost-effective outside of the acute care hospital. Richard, however, knew that these doctors were world-famous orthopedic surgeons and HealthSouth's teaming with them gave us instant credibility. Not only were these men national leaders, they understood the importance of therapy to the patient's successful recovery from surgery and injuries. This was another brilliant move by Richard, as it really elevated HealthSouth's brand as a progressive health care company.

Richard promised the doctors that HealthSouth would build them a new, state-of-the-art hospital replete with a world-class outpatient rehab center. The hospital would specialize in orthopedics, with the understanding that treating sports and work-related injuries were profitable areas of our business. Moreover, these patients made for a great marketing strategy. We soon adopted the phrase, "HealthSouth—getting people back to work, back to play, back to living." From this point forward we did everything we could to align ourselves with orthopedic surgeons who had the most respected sports medicine practice in their communities. Later HealthSouth purchased several other acute care hospitals that specialized in orthopedics.

Until 1994 HealthSouth had grown primarily by expanding its existing facilities, starting new facilities or acquiring units one at a time. This approach had grown the company to about $500,000,000 in revenues by year's end in 1993.

This pattern changed in January 1994 when HealthSouth purchased 73 facilities from National Medical Enterprises (NME). In terms of revenue, this almost doubled the size of the company. During the late 1980's and early 1990 while HealthSouth was growing, so was the entire rehabilitation market. Several companies had started up and followed us to the public market. The investment bankers encouraged us to start buying our competition. They pointed out that consolidation of a new industry is a common phenomenon, and it is usually better to acquire than be acquired. This of course greatly appealed to Richard. In 1994 we acquired ReLife with $220,000,000 worth of HealthSouth stock.

The outpatient surgery center business matured during this growth period by the rehabilitation industry. In 1995 HealthSouth acquired Surgical Health Corporation (SHC) with $155 million of our stock, putting us in a new, but related business. It was outpatient, which meshed with our strategy. Also, many of these patients needed therapy and the same doctors doing the surgery were already referring us patients, so it was a logical fit. HealthSouth now had three main business lines—Inpatient Rehab Hospital, Out Patient Rehab Centers and Outpatient Surgery Centers.

The next major acquisition was eleven rehabilitation hospitals and 12 outpatient centers from a company called NovaCare. These acquisitions and the growth of our existing business pushed us over $1.6 billion in revenues. We were devouring our competition at an alarming rate. However, digesting them was another story.

This short, three-year period when the company went from $500 million in revenues to $1.6 billion was one of great change. Up until this time I had visited all of our locations and knew many of our managers at these facilities. I felt like I had a good working knowledge of the company. In 1990 we had about 3,500 employees, but by the end of 1995 we had over 26,000. The company felt much different. All of our accounting was done from the home office in Birmingham. The task of adding 22,500 employees to the payroll in three years was significant, and amounted to adding over 20 employees everyday for the same period. I felt bad for my payroll department because I could see at times that they were overwhelmed. But, they somehow got it done.

The assimilation of all of these companies from an accounting point of view was horrendous. However, you would have been considered out of your mind to suggest to Richard that the company should slow its growth simply for accounting purposes. After all, you must recall Richard's previous statement that, "The accounting tail is not going to wag the company dog."

Wall Street was somewhat mixed as to the wisdom of our rapid growth. It was Richard's and my job to explain to the analysts and institutional investors why this strategy made sense. Richard and I were the only people at the company who communicated with the Street. I spent much of my time with Richard discussing how we would spin everything. As events (earning releases, acquisitions, Medicare rule changes, news about our competitors, etc.) occurred it was pretty predictable which questions the Street would ask. Richard and I wanted to be sure we were saying the same thing in response to those questions.

The biggest and simplest answer to why we were making all these acquisitions was "Because we could." This may sound flippant, but it fit. Our stock had the highest price/earnings (P.E.) ratio of any stock in our sector. In other words our currency (stock) was more valuable than our competitors. This allowed us to issue stock for their stock and both companies would benefit from the transaction.

It is important to understand how we went about consuming our competition through acquisitions. In order to buyout a company you need to compensate its stockholders. To do this, we primarily used

HealthSouth stock. To further explain how this was done, let me provide a quick lesson in acquisition finance.

Let's say that Company A is earning $1,000,000 annually. It has one million shares outstanding, meaning its earnings per share (EPS) is $1.00 per share. Its stock is selling at $20 per share, giving it a price/earnings (P.E.) ratio of 20.

Company B is also earning $1,000,000 annually. It too has one million shares outstanding, meaning its earnings per share (EPS) is also $1.00 per share. Its stock is selling at $30 per share, giving it a price/earnings (P.E.) ratio of 30.

Company B can buy company A with 800,000 shares of stock for a price of $24,000,000 (800,000 x $30). The value of Company A on the stock exchange is $20,000,000.

The resulting merged company now has $2,000,000 in earnings with 1,800,000 shares outstanding. The earnings per share for the new company is $2,000,000/1,800,000 or $1.11. Moreover, with a P.E. of 30, the new stock should be priced at $33, which does not account for any realized cost savings resulting from the merger.

In this scenario, you can see that it's Pareto-optimal—everyone wins, and that's why these acquisition deals usually happen—the numbers align favorably for both sides. The sellers get more for their company than they would otherwise on the exchange and the acquirers end up holding a single, much larger company, more valuable than the combined worth of the previous two.

As you can imagine, this was a wonderful situation for us. We were able to buy companies with paper (not cash or debt) because the market had put a premium on our stock. Investment bankers are great at identifying these opportunities and making the marriages happen, as they are chiefly concerned with deal-making.

As soon as we announced a merger our phones always began ringing with questions from the Street. They understood the math, but they wanted to know how much costs we could cut after the merger. For example, the merged company did not need two presidents, two CFO's, etc. Also, it was always understood that we could generally improve the operations efficiency of the acquired company and make even more profits. Regarding this, we always tried to guide the Street toward a nice increase in earnings but we had to be careful enough not to let the earnings estimate become unrealistic. However, there was an inherent, related problem.

Richard kept estimates on our existing business unrealistically high. Our "same store" growth was not as good as we were leading people to believe. Richard simply could not bear the thought of the stock dropping significantly. When the analyst coupled our existing earnings with the earnings of the acquired companies they came up with more than we said we could accomplish. This happened because we were masking our core business with these mergers. One might ask, "Was this fraud?" Some might say it was like putting lipstick on a pig. Others on the Street said we were "buying our earnings through acquisitions." I sincerely believe many astute investors understood what we were doing and saw it as financial gamesmanship and not outright fraud. There was certainly much rationalization occurring on our part. "Everyone was doing it," was what we said to ourselves during these acquisitions. Also, it is important to note that all of these numbers were estimates or future earnings, and not hard numbers, so it was by nature understood to be principally inexact.

However, there were other accounting methods that we used while merging the acquired company books with ours. From an ethical point of view, these activities were a little more troublesome. As stated, much of accounting is based on estimates. There were items on the books of the new company that were based on estimates. We changed these estimates to make it easier to book earnings going forward. Estimates for bad debts, reserves for legal expenses and revenue collections were some examples. It was not so much that we made these changes, it was the fact that we did not disclose these changes that was so concerning. Again, one might ask,

"Was this fraud?" You must temper your answer with the caveat that we were dealing with estimates—which in accounting, can always be changed.

Besides the "accounting reasons" there were important business reasons for being the consolidator of the industry. By having a complete spectrum of services in hundreds of locations we could better negotiate with insurance companies, Health Maintenance Organizations (HMO's), large corporations and other payers. Because of the ever-increasing costs of health care in the United States, payers were beginning to aggressively negotiate with providers. Consequently, our sheer volume allowed us to be competitive in this regard.

While these multiple acquisitions increased revenues, they put pressure on our margins. It became increasingly more difficult to keep delivering to the Street the earnings we had led them to believe we could produce. I am not sure that the general public realizes how much influence the company has on the analyst who publishes earnings estimates for a company. The analysts do not make estimates in a vacuum. They seek as much guidance from the analyzed companies as they can acquire. By 1995 and 1996 it was becoming clear to me and others in the company that Richard was allowing the Street to get ahead of what we could really accomplish. His ego—and greed for even more wealth—were out of control.

In hindsight, maybe we were all a little out of control. My salary bonuses and stock options had steadily increased over the maturation years of the company—not nearly as much as Richard's, but at this time I had money I never dreamed of having. All executive compensation decisions were made by Richard. This included his personal compensation package. Richard set the stage years earlier with the Board of Directors that he should be paid what he felt he was worth. In 1985, after completing our first year of operation, Richard submitted to the board pay increases for the company founders. Richard had taken a pay cut to leave Lifemark and start HealthSouth. I cannot recall the exact number of the requested pay hike by Richard at this time, but I do remember that it was big. Richard asked me prior to the board meeting, "Aaron, don't you think I deserve this?" Of course, I said, "Yes." During the board meeting, Richard walked out and left the building. As the board members exited the meeting you could tell it had been a tense round. Richard later shared with me that before he left the building in a semantic fit he told them that they could "run the company themselves" if he was not going to be paid a fair salary. After a short standoff, Richard returned to the board meeting and was granted his requested large pay increase. To the best of my knowledge, Richard was never again challenged by the board about his continued compensation requests.

During these times of unprecedented growth for HealthSouth there were many days in which Richard and I drove to the HealthSouth hanger at the Birmingham Airport, where we kept our fleet of ten company aircraft, to fly to New York City for investor meetings. We normally boarded our Gulf Stream jet—a $25,000,000 plane, at about 7:30 a.m. The stewardesses prepared breakfast as we flew to Teterboro Airport in New Jersey. After landing, a helicopter shuttled us to Manhattan where a waiting limousine took us to the investor meetings. By 5:00 p.m. we were back on the jet, enjoying another meal and cocktails during our ride back to Birmingham, where we would usually arrive no later than 8:00 p.m.

Richard's fondness for displaying wealth peaked when HealthSouth built its new corporate headquarters in 1995. For years Richard had sold investors on the idea that HealthSouth was a lean, cost-effective healthcare provider. He always pointed to the fact that we had no plush offices with fancy chandeliers or thick carpet, and that we were housed in an extremely modest rental space. The new, 200,000 square foot, five-story office building that sat on 85 acres, once completed, was eye-popping. It cost $38 million, and Richard oversaw every step of its construction, including his own trophy room where he hung his many musical accolades. Ironically, the chandelier placed in the Richard M. Scrushy Conference Center was massive and there were dozens of pieces of expensive art— hand-picked by Richard—adorning the walls throughout the building. Also, just like the President of the United States must have his likeness in every Federal building, Richard ordered that a framed color photograph of him be hung in the lobby of every HealthSouth facility. I had no idea how much all of this cost at the time because the line-item construction details were viewed only by Richard.

Times had changed considerably. In the beginning Richard reviewed with me how much we should spend on office furniture and other corporate expenses. Now, he never asked for my input, and I did not dare question his spending, as he had changed in personality. He was at the height of his power.

Beneath the corporate headquarters was a small parking garage for the upper-level management. It became known as the "Bat Cave" in part because our new company logo looked a lot like the Batman symbol. A private elevator that could only be operated with a coded card took us directly to our offices on the building's top floor. Upstairs, there was a private kitchen and dining room adjacent to the executive offices. Richard's office of course had its own private rest room. Richard restricted access to this level. He became extremely reclusive since he had a building and floor plan that would allow him to do so. Furthermore, Richard had surveillance equipment installed throughout the building and implemented a security card system for all employees to control building access as well as access to certain areas within the structure. As a result, the place became eerie.

I had never had the kind of money I earned at HealthSouth. Like anyone, I bought things. I also started a crawfish boil festival, and gave some of the money to charity. I bought the kind of stuff the nouveau rich buy—homes and cars. Unlike Richard, I never really got into boats and airplanes. In the 1990's I owned homes in Birmingham, the New Orleans French Quarter, and several houses on St. George Island in Florida. I drove really nice cars to these homes. Through the years I had two Mercedes, a Boxster, three Lexus, 3 BMW's, a Land Rover, a Jeep and a pickup truck. While this was obviously excessive, the most extravagant expenditure was my neck tie collection. It was the height of my excess.

When Richard and I began traveling to New York City on business we noticed that most of the investment bankers wore a certain brand of neck ties—Hermes. I loved these ties—so much so that by the time I left HealthSouth in 1997, I had accumulated over 300 of them at an average cost of $100 each. Richard had at least twice as many as me. One Christmas, I recall buying each of the men reporting directly to me a Hermes tie as a gift. They had worked hard, and I wanted to get them something nice. A few days after giving the gifts Richard called me into his office and told me how disappointed he was that I had done so. He explained that those ties were our trademark, and by giving these to others below us detracted from that special brand we had forged. Richard seemed to think that Hermes had made ties only for us. Of all the rotten things Richard had said and done through the years, this incident, in particular, personified his selfishness. It really upset me, and still does.

***

Prior to the HealthSouth fraud being headline news in 2003, more people in Birmingham may have known me as the person who started the annual crawfish boil than one of the people who started HealthSouth. Being from Louisiana and having attended LSU in Baton Rouge, I was fond of boiled crawfish. Although it was a practiced South Louisiana tradition, in 1985 in Birmingham few people had ever eaten a single crawfish, much less attended a crawfish boil.

Louisiana is unique. In addition to crawfish boils, there are annual festivals and fairs in cities and towns throughout the state during almost every weekend of the year. Phyllis and I missed boiled crawfish and the many Louisiana festivals when we moved to Alabama. We decided that each spring when crawfish came into season we would have a crawfish boil at our house. The inaugural crawfish boil was at my Mountain Brook home in 1985. We boiled one 40-pound sack of crawfish and had a few friends over to enjoy them with us.

Richard and Karon were there. There was no live music, but I did hear Richard sing for the first time at this party. We had a piano in the living room and to my surprise Richard sat down and started to play and sing. I had no idea that he enjoyed playing music and singing. I asked him how he learned to play the piano. Not surprisingly, he said he had picked it up "from watching his sister take lessons." He seemed to really enjoy performing. It was a side of him I had not seen. Later that evening he told me that one of his lifelong dreams was to have a band.

The next spring we were living in a new house. We moved to Birmingham's south side and there we planned another crawfish boil and house party. We invited mostly HealthSouth employees and people I knew from HealthSouth, like bankers, accountants and lawyers. Phyllis' brother, Bobby, drove from New Orleans with several hundred pounds of mud bugs. I iced down several beer kegs. Richard's newly-formed band, Proxy, played for the first time in my backyard. It was some party. It started at 3:00 p.m. and the police asked us to shut it down at about midnight.

The next year, Proxy played again along with Telluride and several other bands. Within a few years the event, officially touted as "Beam's Crawfish Boil: A Slice of Louisiana," was so popular that a black market developed for the invitations. Amazingly, people with invitations were counterfeiting them and giving them to their friends. As a result, there were dozens and dozens of strangers showing up to the crawfish boil. These were people I had never met. The following year I decided to turn the private party into a public event and raise money for charity.

In 1996 Jack Schaeffer joined me in sponsoring the event. Dr. Schaeffer owned the Birmingham-based Schaeffer Eye Center and at the time was looking for a sponsorship opportunity. It became the Schaeffer-Beam Crawfish Boil, with proceeds benefiting the Leukemia and Lymphoma Society. Today I have no remaining ties to the crawfish boil, but I am proud that Dr. Schaeffer has continued the tradition. Over the years the event moved to Sloss Furnace, the Lakeview area and near downtown. 2009 was the 24th consecutive year it has been held, with tens of thousands attending the event annually.

As a lover of good music, I was always proud of the type of acts the event attracted through the years as its popularity grew. Artists like John Mayer, Rollin' In The Hay, Dr. John, Widespread Panic, Marcia Ball, Warren Haynes, Buckwheat Zydeco, Charmaine Neville and John Mooney, among others, were all featured acts at the Crawfish Boil. In 2009, Snoop Dog was the headliner.

When the event became extremely popular, I could tell that Richard was really annoyed. It was one of the few times that I successfully upstaged him, and he was not happy about it. I spent a ton of foolish money on these parties, but at least the crawfish boil is not remembered as one of the largest frauds the United States has ever seen.

In addition to the crawfish boil, my Hermes necktie collection, cars and homes, my wealth also changed my life in other ways. In 1991

Richard wanted to open a live music club in the Collonnade Strip Mall, next to our corporate offices. He wanted his band Proxy, of course, to be the "House Band." I partnered with Richard and several others to open the night club. I liked the idea because it was the type of business I was around as a child. Like my father, I found the club business exciting. Moreover, just like my father, at times I drank more than I should have. Being the CFO of a New York Stock Exchange company is certainly a full-time job, but I led myself to believe that the "Rock N' Horse," which was the name we gave the place, would not interfere with my real job, since I would not have to run the club. Richard picked a manager to run it for us. I figured I was just going to be an owner, like Richard. By this time Richard and I could go to any restaurant or club in Birmingham and be treated like celebrities. The thought of having my own club in which to play "big shot" appealed to me. Richard and I crunched the numbers and it looked on paper like the Rock N' Horse would be profitable. Unlike HealthSouth, nothing went as planned.

The manager we hired was a total disaster. Richard completely lost interest in the place when the public did not warm to Proxy. The true music lovers in town pretty much blackballed the place because they felt it was a "rich man's club." It quickly became clear that the club would not make money. As a result, I began spending many nights at the club to try and turn things around. Unfortunately, I do not like being around people who drink unless I am also drinking. In hindsight, I should not have put myself in this situation.

Richard asked me to acquire his interest in the business for free if I would agree to be on the lease for the building. I was stupid enough to do it. Things only got worse. The main live music club in Birmingham had always been Louie Louie on the south side of town. I learned the club was for sale and quickly purchased it. I somehow reasoned that this would help me book the bands I needed to make both clubs work. I also believed because Louie Louie had been around for years that it too could be a money maker. In hindsight, my ego was out of control. I wanted to own the most famous and popular live music club in town. While I hired managers for the clubs, they still required a lot of my time, and I was drinking excessively. Night clubs expose you to a lifestyle that can get you into trouble. There were many honky tonk women frequenting both clubs and they almost cost me my marriage. It took me until 1994 to get out of the failing ventures. Little did I know that one day Richard would use my transgressions in the night club business to help discredit me at his trial.

Another unsavory trait that I inherited from my father was gambling. When the Birmingham Turf Club Horse Race Track opened I became a regular customer. One night I got lucky and won $6,000. Later that night the teller I always placed my bets with asked me if I wanted to buy a horse. She was friends with a trainer at the track who wanted to sell one. Just like the day I bought a Mercedes when I was only supposed to buy hamburgers, I bought the race horse. The thoroughbred raced a few weeks later and came in third. It was exhilarating. Later, when the Birmingham track stopped racing horses I sent the horse I purchased to race in Louisiana. I bred the horse several times and actually did okay in the horse business. One of the offspring from that horse actually won a few hundred thousand dollars. My share of its winnings kept me from losing my shirt on the venture like I had in the night club business.

7

Fix the Numbers

"I am Going to Deny Everything"

During the first few years of trading, HealthSouth's stock performed great because our business was strong and Richard was a super pitch man. Richard was absolutely at his best at investor conferences. When he spoke the room was always packed. On many occasions after Richard completed his presentation I watched investors leave the room and go directly to pay phones. There were always computers in the lobby providing up-to-date stock information and quotes. Almost like clockwork, within minutes of these phone calls HealthSouth volume would increase and the stock would inevitably climb a point or two. It was almost like having insider information to know where and when Richard was speaking.

At a breakout session at one of these conferences an investor repeatedly asked Richard the same question by paraphrasing it different ways. After repeatedly answering the question with the same answer, Richard finally told the guy that he "was obviously too stupid to own HealthSouth stock." Richard was always fearless when talking to investors. I was often told in confidence when talking to investors that they liked Richard and me as a team because I was so different than him. Many said that if I were just like Richard they probably would have been reluctant to own HealthSouth stock. I never shared their feelings with Richard. For the most part, however, Wall Street loved Richard's brashness and hard-driving salesmanship.

Richard's brashness of course showed in his management style. Richard managed by intimidation. It's tough to put into words just how brutally nasty Richard could be. Unless you spent time around him and saw it first-hand, it's difficult to understand. One of the misconceptions that many have about Richard is that he is a big man. He is not. He stands only 5' 8" or so, below the average height for males. To compensate for his shortness, Richard had lifts put into all of his designer shoes. He also had hair implants to battle his constant hair loss. But instead of stature, Richard used his facial expressions, his voice and his demeanor to intimidate others.

Richard was always the best villain on Monday mornings. Every Friday, the joke around the office became "Whose turn is it to be in the barrel Monday morning?" One particular Monday morning Richard, like always, gathered the administrative staff for a meeting. To my surprise, Richard started talking about a fishing trip he had taken over the weekend. Richard described a fish he caught, how big it was, and how exciting it was for him to land this huge fish. Richard certainly thought it was great, but to everyone else, it was just another fish story.

A week later, during our regular Monday morning meeting, one of the accountants that reported to me started talking about how he had gone fishing over the weekend, and like Richard, had caught a big fish. He described the fish and how it was huge. Richard did not like this. He had to be the center of attention—it always had to be about him—and no one else. Richard jumped all over the poor guy. Veins popped out of his neck and on his forehead. He was irate. He aggressively admonished the guy. "Shut up! Nobody wants to hear about your damn fish!" Richard yelled, shaking his finger at the fellow. The guy became silent. Richard continued with his barrage, "If you keep that up you'll find yourself doing accounting in the basement!"

It appeared to me that Richard's ever-increasing wealth and ruthlessness made him paranoid. In the mid 1990's Richard hired a personal bodyguard and started carrying a gun in his briefcase. He also purchased a large, vicious German Shepherd watchdog. It was fenced, but it did freely roam his sprawling Vestavia Hills property. The firearm later got Richard into big trouble.

Richard was invited to Washington to visit the White House. He flew to D.C. on one of the HealthSouth planes. After the visit, there were mechanical problems with the HealthSouth plane, which forced Richard to take a commercial airliner home. However, Richard forgot about the gun in his briefcase. He tried to board the plane and did not make it through the security checkpoint. Once the gun was found he was taken to a security room at the airport and detained for some time. Richard tried to explain that it was an honest mistake and he even indicated that he had been in town "visiting with the President." In retrospect, I don't think this revelation helped his case much as he was held for several hours and had to hire an attorney and pay a fine for the imbroglio.

By 1994 my relationship with Richard was changing. During the early years I felt somewhat close to Richard. He and I spent much time together representing the company in New York on Wall Street. He seemed at times to genuinely appreciate my input. However, with the success of the company and Richard's growing wealth and fame as a Wall Street darling he certainly did not seek my input as he had in the past. Furthermore, he was greatly expanding his activities outside of the company. He was learning to fly the company jet airplanes and his band, Proxy, was an ongoing obsession. He had stereo systems installed in the company planes so that we could hear tapes of Proxy performing while we were traveling. If investment bankers traveled with us, they too had to hear the Proxy tapes. Richard would always say, "Don't you think this sounds great?" as he blared the tapes. It quickly got old.

Richard also became active in politics at all levels. He had a tendency to support whoever was in office. He aligned himself with Alabama Governor Guy Hunt. On the national scene Richard courted Speaker of the House Newt Gingrich and a long list of others. We had a lobbying firm looking out for our interests in Washington, D.C. Richard contributed to dozens of politicians' campaigns. Not only did he give his own money, he required all of the upper level management to also contribute to political campaigns. Many times the politicians would come to our corporate office for a breakfast or a lunch meeting. At the end of the speeches Richard would distribute donation checks he collected from everyone. The management, including myself, went along with this odd request because Richard always paid us back for these donations by adding the amounts to our annual bonus checks. Just as Richard had used HealthSouth money to build public monuments bearing his name, he used HealthSouth to accumulate political access and clout.

When Richard had *The History of HealthSouth* written by Jeff Rodengen the forewords of the book were written by United States Senators Orrin Hatch and Thomas Harkin. He was also associated with Tom Daschle, the South Dakota Democrat, J.T. Waggoner, Alabama State Senator, Newt Gingrich, former Speaker of the House from Georgia, Richard Shelby, United States Senator from Alabama, John Breaux, United States Senator from Louisiana, Tom Harkin, United States Senator from Iowa, John Ensign, United States Senator from Nevada, J.C. Watts, former Oklahoma Congressman, Don Siegelman, former Alabama Governor and Billy Tauzin, former United States Congressman, Chair of Energy & Commerce, from Louisiana.

Richard's political connections ran deep and I believe he seriously considered seeking public office. I recall Richard contemplated running for Governor of Alabama. It is a shame he did not do so because it would have been extremely interesting and entertaining. I could imagine Richard telling the people of Alabama that they are "obviously too stupid" to vote for him.

Richard became known as a philanthropist, but he enjoyed giving away HealthSouth's money to become one. Rarely if ever did Richard donate his own money to charitable causes. It was always the company's money. One of his first acts of big charity was the development of the Richard M. Scrushy Public Library in Vestavia, just outside of Birmingham. HealthSouth had purchased a building in Vestavia and the plan was to convert it into a HealthSouth Rehab Center. Richard asked me if I thought it would be a good idea to donate the building to the City of Vestavia for a new public library. He explained that it would be a great public relations move for the company. I attended the dedication ceremony and was surprised to see that the sign in front of the building read, "Richard M. Scrushy Library" and not "HealthSouth Library." I believe this was the first public structure that carried Richard's name; but many more followed, including the satellite Jefferson State College Campus in Birmingham, the Richard M. Scrushy Parkway in Birmingham, the Richard Scrushy Daycare Center, Scrushy-Striplin Field–a baseball complex at Birmingham Southern College, the library at the American Sports Medicine Institute in Birmingham, the Richard M. Scrushy building at the University of Alabama, the Richard M. Scrushy Conference Center, and of course, his own self-monument—a museum constructed at the HealthSouth headquarters in Birmingham devoted to Richard's career and legacy as a health care business icon. Of course, in due time, subsequent to the fraud's revelation, all of these structures and edifices eventually reverted to their original names or changed their names in an attempt to distance themselves from the now-tainted, former, favorite son.

HealthSouth opened doors for Richard and provided opportunities for him that he otherwise would have never had. Through the company's political affiliations he met some of the country's most powerful people. Richard changed his band "Proxy's" name to "Dallas County Line." Proxy was always a running joke, because companies often use proxies to vote on important issues. Simultaneously, Richard replaced some band members with "Nashville pickers," talented musicians from the Oak Ridge Boys and the Sawyer Brown Band, as he was trying really hard to break into the Nashville country music scene.

HealthSouth began sponsoring the popular group "Alabama" as well as hiring Nashville music acts to play for HealthSouth's corporate meetings so Richard could continue to run in those important circles. Among the more noteworthy acts to play for us was Faith Hill. In addition, Richard began associating with acclaimed orthopedic surgeon, Dr. James Andrews—the personal doctor for Bo Jackson, and would often make the HealthSouth plane available to him and his family if they needed it for business, or just for convenience. Dr. Andrews was and remains a pioneer in the field of sports medicine. In addition to his expertise in elbow and shoulder surgery, he is credited with developing the now standard procedure to repair one of the more common sports injuries that occur today--the torn Anterior Cruciate Ligament (ACL Surgery).

Richard was also able to use his status to meet many high profile athletes. I recall in the early 1990's Richard was the personal guest of former Green Bay Packer and two-time Super Bowl MVP Bart Starr at the Super Bowl. Richard sat next to Starr, the Montgomery native, who was hired to speak at HealthSouth events. While these moves by Richard may have seemed questionable to some, in reality it was an ingenious marketing strategy. HealthSouth, by virtue of its association with so many high-profile doctors and athletes, benefited tremendously, because the public saw the company in the same favorable light afforded to these icons of American medicine and sports culture. By doing this HealthSouth's brand became synonymous with success.

Richard even became friends with Troy Aikman, famed former Dallas Cowboy quarterback. Richard even let Aikman use the HealthSouth jets until he felt Aikman was abusing the privilege, and then he quickly cut him off. Richard was truly running with the rich and famous, and more and more he was looking for ways to promote himself and his many growing ventures outside of HealthSouth.

To help promote Dallas County Line Richard hired the brother of one of Sony Records top vice presidents. A job was created for him in our marketing department. Furthermore, HealthSouth began sponsoring a stage at "City Stages," the annual Birmingham music event that is no longer. Of course, Dallas County Line was afforded the opportunity to play self-composed titles like "Honk if you Love to Honky Tonk" during a prime time slot, as a result of this sponsorship. HealthSouth employees were always asked by Richard to attend these sponsored events in which Proxy played. The ritual became known as "purchased applause."

When a reasonable person stepped back and examined what was going on it was easy to see that HealthSouth the corporation was spending money earmarked for publicity that was only benefiting Richard and his many self-aggrandizing pet projects unrelated to HealthSouth.

One of the most disturbing personal ventures of Richard's was G.G. Enterprises. Richard's father worked for many years for National Cash Register (NCR). NCR had a line of personal computers. Richard suggested to me that upon his father's retirement with the company his father was going to become a licensed dealer for NCR. Richard said that he and his dad researched it and discovered that HealthSouth could purchase all of its business office and other computers from NCR cheaper than any price offered by any competitor. Moreover, he added that his father would only recognize a small profit from each computer sold and HealthSouth would be saving money as a result.

I had worked for Richard long enough to know that I could not point out the obvious to him—that this would be viewed as self-dealing. I could tell by the way he presented the overwhelming benefits to HealthSouth that he did not want to hear about it. He assured me that G.G. Enterprise's prices would be reviewed regularly like any other vendor, and at the point it was no longer the best deal for HealthSouth that the company would buy computers elsewhere. In time, this association with Mr. Scrushy (G.G. Enterprises) became a huge problem.

The price of small business and personal computers was falling greatly. Our field managers began comparing G.G. Enterprises' pricing to their own pricing of comparable computers from other companies. Some of these managers, upon discovery, were bold enough as to write letters requesting new computers not from G.G. Enterprises, based on prices quoted and demonstrated performance. Their requests were summarily rejected. Company policy stated clearly that they had to purchase from the preferred vendor. The field managers were incredulous. There was much talk amongst them that the G.G. Enterprises contract had become a troubling moral issue within the company.

At a corporate meeting I was approached by several field managers about G.G. Enterprises. They had already confirmed that the company was owned by Richard's father. They felt that since I was close to Richard I might be able to explain to him how this type of arrangement was hurting the company and could hurt the perception of the company.

I made the decision to talk to Richard about G.G. Enterprises. I decided to talk to him behind his closed door, just him and me. It would have been impossible to persuade him in front of any group. I thought long about how to handle this. I actually believed there was a chance that Richard would realize the severity of the matter and agree to review the pricing with an open mind. I was wrong. Richard listened as I spoke. I could tell by his body language that he did not like what he was hearing. He told me I should not be worried about this, that I had plenty to do, that purchasing was not my job. He insulted me. He said "I did not know what I was talking about;" that "I needed to leave his office;" and to "never bring up the issue again."

It was unbelievable. Richard was at the point financially where he could have easily given has father $10,000,000 to live out his retirement years. It was all so unnecessary. Later, HealthSouth was sued by the Federal Government for $8.2 million over Medicare fraud. The Justice Department claimed that from 1992 to 1997 HealthSouth overcharged Medicare and the Defense Department for equipment and supplies purchased from G.G. Enterprises, a company owned by the parents of HealthSouth's CEO and founder, Richard Scrushy. The government also alleged that HealthSouth fraudulently billed the items at a price that exceeded costs, an important contract stipulation inserted by Medicare. HealthSouth—not G.G. Enterprises, quickly paid the monetary penalty.

However, G.G. Enterprises was not the only venture outside of HealthSouth in which Richard was connected to in some way. There were many others. Richard was either an investor or a principal in the following twelve companies: Source Medical Solutions, 21st Century Health Ventures, Physicians Solutions, MedPartners/Caremark, MedCenter Direct, Integrated Health Services, Capstone Capital, Surgical Health, HealthTronics Surgical Services, Meadowbrook Healthcare Company and Cannongate. One of these companies, Capstone Capital, was an investment company created by Richard, Mike Martin and John McRoberts. Of course, HealthSouth gave Capstone Capital money to invest.

By this time the "pulling the wagon" theme at HealthSouth did not seem to fit like it once did. It was clear that Richard was beginning to be the lone rider on the wagon expecting everyone else to be pulling. Moreover, HealthSouth was quickly becoming a platform for Richard to promote himself. This was made extremely clear at the Monday morning meetings.

The concept of the Monday morning meetings was a good one, I thought. All company vice presidents and selected key management were to attend the meetings. Those attending understood that they should plan their week so that they were not traveling on Monday morning. Each person had three minutes to tell the important things he or she accomplished during the previous week and what their goals were for the coming week. The intent was to give everyone in the room an understanding of what was going on in the company. However, Richard used the meetings as an opportunity to promote himself or whatever it was he wanted to accomplish. He always started the meetings. He never spoke for only three minutes. He never told us what he accomplished the week prior, and he never told us what he would be doing the following week. It was simply his time to assert absolute control. More specifically, it was Richard's time to belittle, berate and publicly embarrass employees for lack of performance, underperformance or just to scare everyone silly into fully buying into the "Pulling the Wagon" mantra. Richard's famous line during these early week sessions was, "Why, that's the stupidest thing I've ever heard!" It was a line he used repeatedly to make an example out of someone.

By 1993 Richard's ability to move the stock solely with his salesmanship had greatly diminished. By this time, investors were driven solely by the numbers we reported each quarter. Furthermore, a lot of the accounting tactics we had formerly used began to show in these numbers. Our receivables were increasing and our reserves for bad debts were decreasing. These were sure signs that our revenues were suspect. In other words, we were booking monies we might never collect. There were now several public companies similar to us that the auditors could use to compare numbers. My job of talking to investors became much more difficult. I discovered that there actually was a threshold to the amount of lipstick you can smear on a pig.

Investors kept focusing on our same store growth, as the increase in revenues for those units opened for over a year. In order to disguise the slowing same store growth we began reporting a city or an entire market as a store. For example, if we opened a second outpatient center in a large city like Atlanta we would report this as growth in the first center. In many cases one manager would manage both centers, so we reasoned that this was all one center. We were careful to never disclose exactly how we calculated the numbers, as all of these weaknesses were better hidden earlier, when we began our merger activities.

Each year when the individual operating units prepared their budgets for the coming year it was apparent there was a gap between what the people in the trenches said they could do and what Richard was promising the Street. Most managers like to sandbag their numbers so that they can be sure to beat them. Thus, much of the eventual gap between estimate and reality can played off as simply part of the process. However, many of our vice presidents knew the gap was getting unrealistic—they just didn't know how ridiculous it already was.

These vice presidents were at the time unable to see the big picture, nor account for growth by acquisitions and the amount of corporate overhead. They did, however, understand the pressure put on them to achieve the ever-growing numbers inside the facilities they managed. Richard was pushing them to create greater revenues while simultaneously cutting costs. Meanwhile, Richard was buying multiple jet airplanes, the company was buying computers from his father, building public monuments in his name and using the HealthSouth check book to finance his failing musical career.

In 1995 we made another public stock offering. By this time we were a much larger company and the road shows were equally larger. The crowds really showed. At these gatherings I was allowed to break out and address investors without Richard present. It was nice to work out from under his wing, so to speak, as he was so incorrigible.

By 1996 it seemed almost hopeless that we could achieve Street expectations. Richard was putting extreme pressure on operations to cut costs, but it was not enough. Our second quarter ended June 30 and the numbers were really weak. Bill Owens, the controller and chief accountant reviewed the numbers with me and we both agreed it was time to report numbers below Street expectations. We had adjusted our reserves for bad debts to the point that any additional decrease would reveal that we would be unable to collect our revenues. After much discussion Bill and I decided to tell Richard the time had come for us to report bad numbers. We felt that after ten years of "making our numbers" we could simply no longer do it. It would have been easier to tell Richard that his singing sucked, but Bill and I were ready to tell him worse. After showing Richard the numbers and telling him we had to report bad numbers, he flatly said, "No."

Bill and I hoped against all odds that Richard would have said, "Okay." We were not so lucky. He asked us the obvious questions, were we sure the numbers were correct and had we made all the accounting adjustments possible. We assured him we had done everything possible. Nevertheless, he answered that we simply could not report the numbers as they were. Richard explained to us what we already knew—that the stock would drop like a rock and every stock holder would be upset. We would no longer be the hero of Wall Street and the rock stars of Birmingham. Our stock options would be worthless and there would be no bonuses paid. Then he told us all the unrealistic, grandiose things he was going to do to turn the company around. He promised he would cut costs and renew our acquisition activities. He assured us the bad quarter was just a hiccup and could be cured. He asked us to do whatever we could to get him through the quarter so that he had time to right the ship. Even in this dark hour Richard was somehow, still convincing. "Fix the numbers," he ordered.

Bill Owens said he could make entries to get the numbers where they needed to be. He said he would make numerous entries below $5,000 each and the auditors would not review them because they were so small. Bill said he was pretty sure he could get us through the yearend audit without those entries being discovered. I did not suggest any other action. I simply did not have the courage to confront Richard. I let myself believe that we would only do this once—we would get it past the auditors and somehow the next quarter would be better.

After we left Richard's office I asked Bill if there was anything he needed me to do. He said no. At this stage of the company's history I did not make accounting entries in the company computer. There really was no way I could assist Bill. I told Phyllis what was happening with the company. She was the only person I talked to about the fraud.

That night I did not sleep well. I knew my life had taken a terrible turn. I just kept thinking, "This is not really happening..." It was an awful feeling. I was miserable. I felt like I crapped my bed and that I would never be able to sleep in a clean one again.

The next day I asked Bill what entries he made and he told me it was not really necessary that I know. That helped a little—but only a little, as I knew it made me no less guilty. Tony Tanner and Richard prepared the news release announcing yet another great quarter of earnings for HealthSouth. I knew it was all a lie.

The next quarter ended in September. Again, our earnings failed to achieve Street expectations. Again, Richard asked us to fix the numbers to give him more time to turn the company around. It was a little easier going down that road the second time. Nevertheless, nothing changed by the end of the year except the size of the fraud. By this time, Bill had brought several others into the circle. He needed help in making so many entries, and I was unsure how many people knew about the fraud. Like before, Bill was "nice" in not including me in the details of who did what among the growing operation in deceit.

Once the audit began I knew Bill was worried. It was extremely scary for me also. I was part of the audit process. I was not attached to as many of the details like Bill and the other accountants were, but I had to answer standard questions by the auditors each year. They posed such questions as "do you know of any material entries that have been made that we may have not reviewed, any serious weakness in internal contracts, any entries that should have been made that were not, any material changes in accounting estimates, etc." Of course, I lied to them. I said no.

As Bill had hoped, we made it through the audit without the fraud being discovered. During the last half of 1996 and early 1997 all suggestions to Richard were that we lower our estimates for earnings in 1997. Of course, these recommendations fell on deaf ears. The problem was of course, much worse now. The true level of earnings that the company was actually achieving was nowhere near what we had just reported and we needed to show earnings at this bogus level. I somehow agreed to give it two more quarters, hoping for a miracle.

But no miracle came. We had to doctor 1997's numbers to achieve earnings estimates. During this time period Richard surprised Bill and I when he said without prompting that if we were ever caught he was going to deny it all. He said, "You guys can do what you want but I want you to know I am going to deny everything." I was not totally sure what he was telling us, or even why, but I gathered that if I blew the whistle I would be in a fight with him. I felt trapped. I mulled my options. They were: Stay and continue with the fraud; be the whistle-blower; seek legal advice; try to get Richard to report bad numbers discontinuing the fraud; or, just leave the company.

My first option was to stay and continue to perpetuate the fraud. However, I was miserable. Every time a friend, family member, investor, employee or anyone told me what a great job I was doing at HealthSouth it tore me up. I knew it was all a lie. Every time I collected my paycheck I knew I did not deserve it. It was hard to do my job because it seemed so pointless. In simple terms all of the joy of my job was gone. This was replaced with the growing fear that I could be charged with a major crime any day. On top of all of this was the fact that Richard was becoming more and more obsessed with himself and he was not cutting back on the way he spent company money.

My second option was to become a whistle-blower. This option reeked uncertainty. The world would certainly know and there would be hell to pay for it all but I had no idea of how it would play out for me. I knew there was a big chance Richard would turn it all on Bill and me. He could say he never made any entries on the books and simply deny he told us to do so. I was physically afraid of what Richard might do. He carried a weapon at all times and had bodyguards and watchdogs—he was a serious character and I knew he was capable of violence. I was not. The anger I had seen Richard display for things much less consequential than this was alarming. But this was different—it was Richard's livelihood. I knew he would fight hard for it and that he might be capable of doing anything to protect his millions and avoid jail time.

My third option was getting legal advice. I thought hard about this option. I certainly had a legal problem if anyone ever did. But the more I thought about it I felt it would turn out much like option two. Even with the second option I would still need legal advice.

My fourth option was to change Richard. This was not going to happen. I tried before and I knew it was irrational. There was no changing Richard Scrushy.

After much deliberation I decided to just leave the company and hope for the best. I had accumulated a fair amount of wealth and felt I could retire with the funds I had. Under different circumstances I would never have walked away from a job paying me $500,000 a year. I was only 54. But, the money was not worth it. I really did need a greater net worth to retire so young, but I knew this was my best option. If I live well into my eighties I'll probably wish I had saved a little more and spent a little less.

When I told Richard I wanted to retire he was not pleased. He told me he thought I was making a mistake. I cannot remember how it came about but I was able to convince Richard to give me a founder's retirement plan. Richard agreed that the company would pay me $75,000 a year for the rest of my life and I could keep all of my benefits, including medical insurance. He believed this was justified because I was a founder. He said he wanted to put the plan in place so that future retirement by other founders would be covered. I was surprised that Richard would willingly offer this. I felt that it could have been viewed by him as hush money. Richard never said that he hoped that it would keep me quiet about the fraud, but one can only guess what he was thinking. Nevertheless, putting the plan in place for his future benefit was typical Richard. I wanted out, and was glad to be getting from Richard what he offered.

The company ran a news release about my retirement. The plan was for me to leave at the end of the year, but Richard changed his mind and asked me to leave in September. I was more than happy to leave at the earlier date.

Mike Martin, company treasurer at this time, knew about the fraud. I knew Mike hoped to one day have my job. He told me as much. Mike had already been working with Richard and me at investor conferences and was up to speed on how to talk to the Street. I began turning over my duties to him as soon as the news release was sent. The general public and my friends were a little surprised that I was retiring at the young age of 54. I assured everyone that it was time for me to go. I told them I had the funds to do it and just wanted to slow down and enjoy life.

2,000,000 Shares

Common Stock

All of the shares of Common Stock offered hereby are being sold by HEALTHSOUTH Rehabilitation Corporation (the "Company"). Prior to this offering, there has been no public market for the Common Stock of the Company. See "Underwriting" for information relating to the method of determining the initial public offering price.

The Common Stock offered hereby involves a high degree of risk. See "Risk Factors".

THESE SECURITIES HAVE NOT BEEN APPROVED OR DISAPPROVED BY THE SECURITIES AND EXCHANGE COMMISSION NOR HAS THE COMMISSION PASSED UPON THE ACCURACY OR ADEQUACY OF THIS PROSPECTUS. ANY REPRESENTATION TO THE CONTRARY IS A CRIMINAL OFFENSE.

	Price to Public	Underwriting Discounts and Commissions (1)	Proceeds to Company(2)
Per Share	$6.50	$.455	$6.045
Total (3)	$13,000,000	$910,000	$12,090,000

(1) For information regarding indemnification of the Underwriters, see "Underwriting".

(2) Before deducting expenses payable by the Company, estimated at $435,000.

(3) The Company has granted the Underwriters a 30-day option to purchase up to 300,000 additional shares of Common Stock solely to cover over-allotments, if any. See "Underwriting". If such option is exercised in full, the total Price to Public, Underwriting Discounts and Commissions and Proceeds to Company will be $14,950,000, $1,046,500 and $13,903,500, respectively.

The Common Stock is offered by the Underwriters as stated herein, subject to receipt and acceptance by them and subject to their right to reject any order in whole or in part. It is expected that delivery of such shares will be made through the offices of Robertson, Colman & Stephens, San Francisco, California on or about October 1, 1986.

Robertson, Colman & Stephens
Drexel Burnham Lambert

Alex. Brown & Sons
Incorporated

The date of this Prospectus is September 24, 1986

Figure 1 HealthSouth Initial Stock Offering

Figure 2 Richard Scrushy in "Proxy"

Figure 3 Founders of HealthSouth on floor of Wall Street

Figure 4 Richard Scrushy with "Proxy" at our First Crawfish Boil in our backyard

Figure 5 Aaron & Richard at 1993 Crawfish Boil

Figure 6 Dennis Douglas, Weston Smith, Bill Owens, and Aaron Beam
at Vulcan Run

Figure 7 Crawfish Boil at Sloss Furnace

Figure 8 Crawfish Boil in the Lakeview Area

Figure 9 Richard Scrushy and Mike Martin

Figure 10 Richard's third marriage and Leslie's second

Figure 11 Football Field at Beam Acres

Figure 12 Auction ad for Beam Acres

Figure 13 Richard Scrushy

Figure 14 Richard Scrushy on "60 Minutes

Figure 15 Weston Smith

Figure 16 Bronze Statue after Indictments

Figure 17 Birmingham Road Sign

Figure 18 Graffiti

Figure 19 Richard's defense Attorney Jim Parkman

Figure 20 Richard Scrushy in front of the courthouse

Figure 21 Leslie and Richard celebrate first HealthSouth trial

Figure 22 Richard Scrushy and Former Alabama Governor Don Seigelman

Figure 23 Richard Scrushy at Civil Trial

Figure 24 Richard Scrushy's Lake Martin home

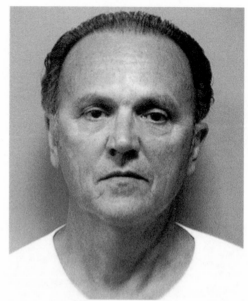

Figure 25 Richard Scrushy's mug shot

Figure 26 My new career

8

Finding Fairhope

"I Build a Football Field"

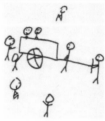

Phyllis and I had always been fond of the Fairhope, Alabama area in South Alabama. We had often talked about where we might retire some day. We had considered going back to Texas or Louisiana, but Fairhope was certainly in the mix. The culture, food and climate in Lower Alabama have much in common with South Louisiana, making it an enjoyable place to live. Also, with Interstate 10 nearby, we could always get to Louisiana in just a couple of hours. Fairhope had recently been named by *USA Today* as one of the "Best Retirement Communities in the USA." We began looking for land in Baldwin County, where Fairhope is located. We wanted to buy acreage and build our dream home. We wanted it to be the last home we owned.

We found 25 acres on Alabama State Highway 98 near the Fish River Bridge. It was exactly what we wanted. A couple of years passed before we built on the land. The real estate market in Greystone Golf and Country Club where we lived in Birmingham was weak and we had few offers on our place, which we needed to sell in order to build our dream home in Fairhope.

During these early retirement years Phyllis and I spent a lot of time at our beach house on St. George Island, Florida, at our condominium in the New Orleans French Quarter, and traveling. Our primary residence remained our Birmingham home, even though it was on the market.

In early 1998, six months after leaving the company, I was no longer considered an insider by the Securities and Exchange Commission. Therefore, I was free to exercise the HealthSouth options I had. I sold nearly all of my remaining stock. I did not see the company having a bright future as long as Richard was riding in the wagon. One thing about selling large shares of stocks is that when you receive the proceeds, if you are smart, you immediately pay the government its share in income taxes. I always paid my taxes, and I used to joke to Phyllis as I wrote some of those larger checks that I hoped the government at least named an aircraft carrier after me, because I wrote them checks totaling many millions of dollars through the years.

I continued to be active in the annual crawfish boil with Dr. Shaeffer, but I had no contact with HealthSouth. I was glad to be gone and did not want to look back. There was one exception, however. In 1999 Richard called me and asked me to have lunch with him at HealthSouth's corporate office. During the lunch Richard asked me to come back to work. He said the company was doing great and was making its numbers. He said he needed me to help keep growing the company. He assured me that the future for HealthSouth was bright. I declined his offer. I never even for a nanosecond considered it. I was done with that.

I threw myself into improving the 25 acres Phyllis and I purchased in Baldwin County, Alabama. The property was devoid of any man-made structures and about 75% of it was overgrown with brush and wild plants. It was impossible to drive a vehicle on the land. There was a small pond, probably a little more than an acre, at the back left corner of the plot. Nearly seven acres at the front of the property were planted with over 100 mature pecan trees.

Phyllis and I decided to build a barn with living space above the ground level. Our plan was to live in the barn while we built our retirement home. The barn's floor plan was simple—one large room with a kitchen/dining area at one end and a bathroom/closet area at the other. The structure was all wood—it contained not a single piece of sheet rock. It was nice and it served us well until the house was completed.

We decided to place the house in the virtual center of the property. There was a large area behind the house that was devoid of trees. I was unsure what to do with it. I measured it and realized it was 150 yards in length and 80 yards wide. For some reason the thought came to me that a football field would fit inside this part of the property. The idea stuck.

I had hoped to keep a large green space on the property that could be used as a place to play ball, throw a Frisbee, hold a live music event or maybe even a crawfish boil. The more I thought about how to use the space, the more a football field made sense. When I told Phyllis I wanted a gridiron behind the house she didn't appear to give it much credence. She didn't realize that I really wanted a football field.

Once finished the field was special. It was to me, anyway. It was official size, complete with regulation end zones. A retaining wall along the length of the field on the side closest to the house was necessary. The wall was about seven feet tall and I had it adorned with the LSU Tiger logo. The goal posts were also regulation sized and I purchased the same padded wraps that are used in Tiger Stadium in Baton Rouge. Moreover, the turf was Bermuda grass, Tifway 419, also the same strain used at LSU.

The football field ended up costing more than I anticipated, but it was so much fun. One of the bigger expenses I overlooked was that the turf required a $25,000 Reel mower. Also, the field had to be cut every three days during the growing season so that the mower would not clog. I did not mind, as I was retired and enjoyed being outdoors working on my property.

I built a music stage about fifty feet from one end of the football field. By design, I had more electric power on the stage than I had at the house. The first time I booked a band to play on the stage the manager of the band was worried I would not have enough power for their equipment. I flatly told him to worry about something else. When the band showed and saw the power grid I had, the manager said, "Wow! The Rolling Stones could play here!" My experience from hosting the Birmingham crawfish boils through the years served me well.

It was 2001 before we finally sold our Birmingham home. We took a huge loss on the transaction, but we were glad to finally begin constructing our home on the Fairhope property. Before we began building the house I had to build a tennis court, a basketball court and a two-bedroom guest cottage. At this juncture Phyllis told me that I could not build anything else or buy any more play things until she had her house. She had a good point.

I wanted to build a much smaller house than the one we had in Birmingham. However, Phyllis wanted more house than I did, but I had sort of lost my mind building out the rest of the grounds. As a result, I was in a weak negotiating position. The house eventually grew to have a pool and pool house, an upstairs apartment, and a wine cellar added to the original blueprints.

After nearly two years of construction, the house was completed. We intended to build a home where we could entertain on a grand scale. Phyllis and I always enjoyed hosting parties. During the short time that we lived there we had several crawfish boils, a fundraiser for charity, several rugby matches, a South Alabama Club football practice, a practice for the semi-professional Mobile Wizard football team and a great open house party before the news of the fraud finally broke.

One of the annual crawfish boils we had occurred in 2002, the year prior to LSU winning the national championship in football. LSU's Offensive Coordinator, Jimbo Fisher, now at Florida State and Defensive Coordinator Will Muschamp, now at the University of Texas, attended the party and were guest speakers. I invited Head Coach Nick Saban, but he did not make the trip. When I had an opportunity to talk one-on-one with Fisher and Muschamp I asked if Coach Saban might attend the event in the coming years. They politely said he would not come. They also assured me that they would return, and would be much more entertaining than Coach Saban. I was impressed with both men. Coach Fisher is the head coach in waiting at Florida State and Coach Muschamp will make in the foreseeable future some school a great head coach.

Phyllis and I planned a really big party to celebrate our open house in the fall of 2002. HealthSouth was firmly behind me, as I seldom thought about what I had left. More than five years had passed and Phyllis and I had developed an entirely new circle of friends. Most of these people knew little of HealthSouth. Our property was less than half a mile from "Lulu's Sunset Grill," the place owned and operated by Lucy, the sister of the famed renegade crooner, Jimmy Buffet. On many afternoons I would tire of cutting grass at Beam Acres (it was the place to be) and I would drive my John Deere Gator to Lulu's for a little Southern-style R&R. If Phyllis needed me, she knew where to call, as Lulu's was one of my all-time favorite hangouts. I was such a regular that Phyllis and I could not go there without seeing someone we knew. It was much like Lou's Pub in Birmingham, except it had great food and live music. But the best part was that it was only a five-minute "Gator ride" away. The close proximity to Lulu's reinforced my belief that I had picked the perfect place to build a retirement home. Sadly, Lucy lost her lease on the property and subsequently built a huge new Lulu's in Gulf Shores. The old Lulu's was like a country store and the new Lulu's is like a Wal-Mart. It just isn't the same.

The Open House party was great. Terrance Simien from Lafayette, Louisiana played his accordion and special brand of Zydeco music on the stage at the back of our property. I had become good friends with Terrance during our Birmingham crawfish boil days. Phyllis and I invited our families and about 100 other people. I invited many of the people I had worked with at HealthSouth, including Richard Scrushy. I later heard from my electrician, who had done work for Richard at his Ono Island home that Richard planned to attend. However, no one from HealthSouth showed. Knowing what I know now about the continued fraud subsequent to my departure from the company, I am sure no one at HealthSouth was in a partying mood. But, at this time I was clueless of the volcano that would soon erupt.

9

Weston Smith's Take

"The Family"

After I left the company in late 1997, it began almost a six-year period for me in which I knew nothing of the goings on at HealthSouth. The information that follows regarding this time was related by Weston Smith, a friend and former HealthSouth colleague.

Previously a health care auditor specializing in reimbursement with *Ernst & Young*, Weston began working for HealthSouth in 1987 as Reimbursement Director after Richard fired his predecessor when he believed the guy was having sex with Richard's secretary; so he was moved into a back office with little hope for advancement. Weston eventually rose to my position after I left—one of five to hold the CFO spot after I departed.

When I called Weston in early 2009 and told him I was writing a book about HealthSouth, I told him that he would be of great assistance toward filling the gap between when I left and when the fraud eventually broke. Weston is a great guy. We always got along, and he immediately agreed to help me. Weston's comments are interesting because he not only connected the dots, but he also provided a much different perspective on Richard's vindictive, ruthless leadership style, as he was not a founder of the company, and was more subject to Richard's daily cruelty than I was as CFO.

Weston recalled things that I never really took stock in, like the fact that each office within the guarded HealthSouth headquarters had either a window to the hallway, or a door, but not both. The logic was that Richard could always keep an eye on everyone. If an office could not accommodate a window, then it did not have a door. Of course, there was one exception--Richard's office had no window and a door.

Weston said that one day after I had left the company he was working on the only HealthSouth copier in the copy room. He said Richard unexpectedly walked in and asked why there was a phone line hanging loosely from the ceiling. He replied that he had no idea. He said that Richard went in to one of his classic tirades—veins bulging—and shouted that the "offices could be bugged!" and that, "someone could be listening to them right now!" He said that he felt Richard's paranoia only grew worse over the years leading to the fraud's revelation.

Weston said that during the time after I left, the infamous Monday morning meetings became increasingly more outrageous. Scrushy loved to tell the business world how productive these meetings were, and how it kept him in tune with everything that was going on and how it was an excellent source of communication from the line folks to management. In fact, he once had the local *Fox* affiliate tape the meeting for one of their powder puff pieces on HealthSouth's favorite son.

The officers resented the public beatings that Richard would administer during the Monday morning meetings, so in an effort to please the master their ongoing reports became more dramatic and less real. The outrageous commentary people made was only met with Richard's bored silence, until of course his pet departments reported. It all made a nice presentation for Richard, though. His table was adorned with a sterling silver ice bucket filled with *Dasani* bottled water and *Diet Cokes*. His security guards, dressed in black suits, white shirts and dark ties, always hovered nearby, whispering often in to their wired sleeves. The guards always escorted him to and from his office in an effort to keep people away from him. It was all a pompous show. Weston said that there were many times that he simply wanted to stand up during a Monday morning meeting and say

"Last week I committed securities fraud for Richard, and if I want to keep my job, this week I'll do the same."

During one of the more strange spring Monday morning meetings, Richard apparently went on a rant about how everyone wasn't working hard enough, how they weren't productive, how they weren't getting to work on time, and how they didn't stay late enough. It was one of Richard's classic blow-ups where his face turned beet red, his eyes clouded dark and his eyelids twitched uncontrollably. Strangely, later that week, on Wednesday, Richard announced that on Friday they would have a "company motorcycle ride." He said that anyone who had a bike should ride it to work on Friday, and at lunch they would all leave work for an "afternoon ride." It is worth noting that it was during this Friday afternoon motorcycle ride that Richard unveiled to the HealthSouth community that he and his new friend, Leslie, were a couple. Leslie hopped on the back of Richard's motorcycle that afternoon, and formally began what can still be considered, in the least--a wild ride.

In our many conversations Weston shed light on HealthSouth's half-hearted attempts toward due diligence during the accelerated acquisitions phase of the late 1990's and early 2000's. During this period the company acquired numerous inpatient rehabilitation hospitals, outpatient rehab centers, ambulatory surgery and imaging centers. Just as in previous years, the precipitous growth presented an enormous challenge to integrate so many new entities within a short period of time. Weston participated in many of the due diligence trips—basically an internal auditing process that the buyer and seller go through which seeks to determine the true financial and operational strength of companies. However, Weston explained that HealthSouth did only cursory due diligence work, as Richard only wanted due diligence performed at a level that was substantive enough to, as he put it, "paper the files." It seemed that no matter what problem was uncovered regarding the target company during these investigations, none were great enough to call off the deal or seriously impact the offering price. He said that Richard's response to poor findings was, "We have to do this deal—because if we don't, someone else will, and then we'll have to compete against them." Weston

- 106 -

said that during one such trip to Miami he called Richard to report unsettling target-related findings. Richard briefly listened, and then interjected, "You guys are smoking dope down there, aren't you?" He said they were ordered to complete their work and that the acquisition was announced shortly after they returned.

Weston realized all along what I did--that they were using the acquisitions to mask HealthSouth's core problems. The logic was that the true value of the deals wouldn't be revealed, and that the synergies of the deal or additional revenues could be used to carry some of HealthSouth's shortfalls. This scheme didn't work though, because many of the acquisitions were conducting their own book-cooking operations, which meant that they not only continued to falsely prop up HealthSouth numbers, but also the numbers of the new acquisitions in order to meet the expectations of Wall Street and Richard. The underlying problems with the acquired facilities weren't completely understood until we owned them, because the due diligence was so weak from the onset.

On a typical due diligence trip there were not many areas that were intensely audited, for fear that if we asked the target company for certain information, they would ask the same from us. It worked both ways—as providing information could possibly reveal HealthSouth's own accounting problems. Many of the investment bankers that the company used in these deals were accommodating about this problem. They typically provided a checklist of information that needed to be gathered, and to sensitive areas Weston and the rest would say with a wink, "We can't ask for that." The understanding was clear: Questions that should have been easy to answer would not be asked. If the other side pushed for answers to the sensitive questions, the bankers effectively steered them away or berated them for asking those questions of such a "respectable" company.

Weston explained that as the years after my retirement rolled along, actual and reported numbers grew farther and farther apart. The fraud became so bad that by 2002-2003 the company was paying more in Federal income taxes on its reported profits than it was actually making in true net income. Wall Street and Richard had growth expectations each year, so annually they had to grow numbers which were artificially overstated. It was a classic snowball rolling down a mountain. However, the schemes to overstate the financial statements were simplistic. There were not any exotic special purpose entities like at Enron; the HealthSouth fraud was little more than fraudulent debits and credits. It was massive, of course, and required the work of many, but at its foundation, it was quite simple.

Accounting is a series of two-sided entries. There is a debit and a credit. An accounting entry is usually an entry to the income statement with a corresponding entry to the balance sheet. The entries must balance. In its simplest form, income to a company is credited to the income statement as revenue, and the corresponding debit is added to the balance sheet as accounts receivable. In essence, the multibillion dollar fraud was committed by overstating income (the credits) on the income statement, and overstating corresponding amounts (the debits) on the balance sheet.

The initial fraud was perpetrated by understating the portion of billings that a healthcare entity is not typically paid, known as contractual adjustments and bad debts. These items reduce net revenues. As the contractual adjustments and bad debts are understated, the revenues of the company are overstated. On the other side of the financial statements, on the balance sheet, the accounts receivable reserves must be reduced. This has the effect of overstating net accounts receivable, but in this example, provides the balance of debits and credits necessary to perpetuate the fraud.

As HealthSouth's numbers grew, the complication of finding places to park overstatements on the balance sheet became more difficult. They simply could not continue to just understate the accounts receivable reserves, because before long the reserves would dwindle to zero. In order to address this problem, a group of people who were involved with the details of the fraud met at the end of each quarter to discuss strategies on how to continue, and more importantly, to conceal the crime. Bill Owens thought it was cute to call the group "The Family." At the end of a quarter, Bill would call a "family meeting" and we would sit around a table and hash out the accounting they felt was necessary to meet Wall Street's and Richard's expectations. The "family" label also became handy to Richard for year-end merits, bonuses and stock options, as "family" members were always rewarded for their relative importance.

According to Weston, when the family met at the end of each quarter to discuss how to prop up the company's earnings, the shortfall was described as "the hole." A place that fraud could be parked or shifted was called "dirt." The participants in the meeting would put together a plan of how much money would go where on the income statement or balance sheet until the earnings were at the level Richard required. The conspirators then had to make a series of journal entries to place misstatements on the financials of the 1,000 or more HealthSouth locations. Moreover, the participants also had to craft ways to get the work past the auditors.

For example, the person responsible for supporting the reasonableness of contractual allowances or cost report receivables had to be intimately familiar with what they could or couldn't get past the auditors. As time progressed, this exercise became exponentially more difficult. This was so because the contractual allowances had been reduced so many times that the growth in accounts receivable days was being noticed by analysts. The "policies" regarding the recording of receivables and allowances, as reported to the auditors, changed with unusual frequency. In order to create dirt for the holes on the income statement, nearly every line item of the balance sheet became fictitious. Many of the debits on the balance sheet were posted as fixed assets. Literally thousands of assets were created that did not exist. Nearly every line item on the company's balance sheet was misstated, from inventory, to prepaid expenses, notes receivable, accounts receivable and liabilities.

To complete the financial statements for earnings releases, it took approximately 120,000 fraudulent journal entries *per quarter*. As you can imagine, this was extremely labor-intensive. Furthermore, the cash balance was extremely overstated. At one point HealthSouth recorded

$320 million in cash on the books, but in reality had only $10 million in the bank. That had to be one of the biggest shell games ever committed to sneak it past the auditors.

There were many accounting games played by the "Family." Richard's Gulfstream jet owned by the company was sold to a leasing company for over $30 million, and was subsequently leased back for about $300,000 per month for the same jet. The accounting was absolutely reckless. They were lying outright, and wrong for doing it, but it was the only way the company could continue to report the numbers Richard Scrushy demanded.

The fraudulent statements became a beast of their own. For example, overstating fixed assets meant that future depreciation expense had to be taken, and that created further earnings problems down the road. Property taxes had to be paid on these assets. A small closet of inventory at an outpatient center, worth several hundred dollars at most, would be valued at several thousand dollars on the books. Since the fraud was being posted at the end of every quarter, anyone with access to the books could easily see the roller coaster track of earnings at each facility.

Many facility controllers and administrators turned a blind eye to the fraud because it enabled them to meet their budgets and become eligible for greater bonuses and stock option awards. During their subsequent year's budget presentations though, they would describe the quarterly adjustments as "gifts" in which they should not have to budget. The problem with facility people asking questions about their financials became so acute that HealthSouth corporate finally stopped giving them detailed financial statements. Instead, they expected them to run their operations on a few doctored excel spreadsheets. In response, many of the locations began running their own internal financial statements just to track where they really were. The annual reports of the company became a complete work of fiction. For example, since revenues were overstated, then the underlying patient days, or outpatient visits, would have to also be overstated, creating a veritable Pandora's Box in describing the results from operations. Elaborate discussions were crafted detailing our operations, and glowing earnings results were subsequently released to the unsuspecting financial world.

Weston said that the quarterly earnings release calls changed little in the years after I left. An announcement would be made of the date and time of the conference call, and interested analysts and investors would call in. Richard read the body of the earnings release, and the CFO or treasurer would typically read key operating statistics. Because of the fraud, these numbers were a complete work of fiction. The call would then be opened up for questions. The questions would always follow the same pattern. Analysts who were friendly to the company would ask softball questions, or even prepared questions that were given to them by the company. These shills were always given preferential treatment, and were always cued first during the question and answer session. Because the questions were soft, Richard spent much time answering them. As the questioning continued, they of course had to field legitimate ones from concerned investors. Richard became more brief and evasive, and he would frequently end the calls for various reasons, like his "busy schedule."

Weston said he remembers in particular one quarterly call in 2001. The actual numbers were dreadful, but of course the company reported numbers that met Wall Street expectations. Nevertheless, Richard was excellent on the call. His presentation was strong, his answers to questions were articulate, and he really made a strong presentation. After the call, Bill Owens and Weston stayed behind while the others left. Richard looked at both of them and asked, "OK, what *really* happened this quarter?"

As stated, Richard was not only earning great money in salary, bonuses and generous stock options from HealthSouth, he also earned additional salaries, bonuses and stock options from his various Board of Director positions he held with other companies. While I was certainly comfortable, I had nowhere near the amount of wealth Richard had accumulated. I heard that Richard told friends from Selma that he "Was going to make it big or go broke trying." Making it big for Richard meant not only making big money—it meant spending it as well—and spend he did. Richard amassed a cadre of luxurious homes, water craft, jet airplanes automobiles and other gaudy excesses.

By April, 2003, according to tax records, Richard had six homes registered in his name in both Alabama and Florida. The most luxurious of these was a 11,000 square foot beach house in Palm Beach, Florida, which Richard purchased in 2001. Its assessed market value was listed at $11 million. Built in 1998, Richard's 14,000 square foot Lake Martin home, lake/boat house and surrounding lots—which neighbors referred to as "the world's largest La Quinta Inn" because of its Spanish style architecture, was valued at $5 million. A 2.5 story, 16,000 square foot Vestavia Hills (Birmingham) home—with 7 bedrooms and a swimming pool, built in 1956, was valued at $2.2 million. Richard had two other Vestavia Hills homes listed at $300,000 and $125,000. Richard's sixth home at Orange Beach, Alabama—was a 5,000 square foot, two-story, three-bedroom, three-bath home on Ono Island valued at $669,200.

Richard also had three other properties—a farm in Montgomery County valued at $125,000, a skating rink in Vestavia Hills valued at $1.25 million and a two-story office building in West Palm Beach, Florida valued at $1 million.

Richard loved water crafts, according to tax records, he had seven. They included: A 35-foot Ocean Racer, a 92-foot yacht named "Chez Soiree,'" a 36-foot fiberglass recreational sport, two 30-foot fiberglass Hacker Pleasure Crafts, and a 37-foot "Top Gun" cigarette sport boat.

Richard also loved jet airplanes. In addition to his HealthSouth fleet of 12 jets, known affectionately by company insiders as "Air Birmingham," Richard personally owned two aircraft—a 1998 Aviat Husky A1A Seaplane and a 1998 Cessna 208 14-seater prop plane. The company jets were kept in a glistening multimillion dollar hanger at the Birmingham airport. The hanger was also a convenient place for Richard to keep his two personal sea planes. The waste was so pronounced that the jets soon became referred to individually by the executives who used them the most.

In addition to the Gulfstream V, known affectionately as "Richard's plane," Bill Owens anointed a new Cessna Citation X jet as "his," and the other jets became coined with each division president's name. It was truly a time of nauseating excess.

Somehow though, this wasn't enough for Richard. It was during this time that the company had to lay off a number of employees. Many good, hard working people, who needed a bi-weekly pay check lost their jobs. One week after the layoff, Scrushy took delivery on a $6 million Sikorsky helicopter. It was completely customized to Richard's specifications, including adornment of the HealthSouth corporate colors and logos. A hilltop on the corporate campus was graded and converted into a helipad. Along with the hiring of two pilots, the company had to hire a mechanic just to service the chopper.

Jim Bennett, who at the time was the company's COO, told Richard that it did not look good for the company to have something like this flying around Birmingham in such close time proximity to the layoffs. Richard became furious with Jim, and he really let him have it for saying such a thing to him. Richard continued to berate Jim behind his back. Weston said he vividly recalled Richard's related rant, "Jim just doesn't get it! When people see a helicopter fly in, they should be happy. It means that things are happening. It's not just a helicopter, its progress!" Jim never quite recovered from his penchant for honesty, and was, like many before him, run off by Richard within the year.

The helicopter was the icing on the cake in terms of waste within the aviation department, or as Richard referred to it, his personal "air force." The Sikorsky helicopter was frequently used for Richard's family's personal weekend trips to nearby Lake Martin or for shopping trips to Atlanta by his third wife, Leslie. Richard even occasionally used it to go to work from home. When Lloyd Noland Parkway was renamed "Richard M Scrushy Parkway," Richard flew across Birmingham for the ribbon cutting so that he could show off his new toy to the assembled dignitaries. By comparison, the Governor of Alabama rode up from Montgomery in a Ford, but Richard had to fly across town in his Sikorsky helicopter.

On the few occasions that he rode in the helicopter, Weston said he was amused to see that it was full of *Cosmopolitan* and *Glamour* magazines. He added, "I suppose a person has to have something to read when flying to Atlanta via Birmingham."

And of course, there were the cars--37 of them in all, including a $135,000 bulletproof BMW and a $250,000 Lamborghini Murcielago.

Richard's sprawling Lake Martin weekend getaway was where he enjoyed his sport boats and jet skis. However, his lakeside neighbors suffered as a result. Richard loved to run his boats—especially his favorite cigarette, "Top Gun," full throttle on the normally placid lake. When he did it always created a huge wake that rocked the many moored pleasure boats and jet skis along the private piers. Richard was so hated for this that his neighbors often threw beer bottles and cans at him as he whizzed by. Still others always felt it appropriate to extend their middle fingers when he made his way into their part of the lake.

In order to have ample fuel to run these gas-thirsty water toys, Richard needed lots of gas. He tired of having to run to the station to fill a temporary tank. He wanted his own gas station. In order to have what he wanted, he needed a large, underground gas tank—the kind all gas stations have.

Richard ordered an extremely large, submersible tank. The day it arrived via 18-wheeler at the entrance to his gated Lake Martin community, the guard at the front entrance did his job and denied the delivery, as it was not approved. The neighborhood association would have never allowed it, even if Richard had gone through the proper protocols, but of course, Richard always did things his own way. When Richard's handlers were notified by the 18-wheeler driver's company that the gas tank's delivery was being denied, they informed Richard, and he went ballistic. Richard hired attorneys to threaten to sue the development's neighborhood association, but in the end they realized it was fruitless. Needless to say, Richard never got his own gas station near the pristine lake. I'm sure it still irks him to this day because he really thrived on getting what he wanted.

In 1998, two years after I left the company, Richard made *Business Week's* list of the country's highest-paid CEO's after pulling in more than $100 million in bonuses and salaries and more than $90 million in stock options. The ever-increasing wealth and fame only seemed to make him want more. Furthermore, Richard's behavior apparently only became weirder as time passed.

At this time Richard was seemingly bored with the company, evidenced by the fact that he was spending more time on pursuits non-related to HealthSouth, and more closely related to the gratification of his ego. For instance, he spent at least $1 million to fully bankroll his young teenage female glamour band called "Third Faze," which at their brief zenith opened for mega teen star Britney Spears. Furthermore, Richard allegedly paid for breast augmentation for the budding young vocalists. HealthSouth's Board of Directors even approved Richard's dubious request to give $250,000 stock options to the head of *Sony Records*, Tommy Moltola, who predictably later signed Third Faze to a record deal.

After his mother died in 2002, Richard seemed to abandon all logic in his company decision-making. He hired former "Wonder Years" child actor Jason Hervey, who played Wayne, the older brother on the popular weekly television program during the late 1980's and early 1990's, to help him with a radio show. Eventually, Richard named Hervey Senior Vice President of Marketing and Communications for HealthSouth, even though he was not qualified for the position; and was married to a former adult film star, Angel Hart. Predictably, Hervey's hiring caused a great uproar among the HealthSouth ranks, who felt Richard was only stroking his ego by "paying" Hervey to hang out with him. In a related aside, Hervey later, after the fraud broke, sued HealthSouth for $300,000 in salary and $100,000 in stock options to honor the cushy contract Scrushy gave him which stated he would receive $300,000 per year for three years. HealthSouth later settled out of court.

According to Weston, after Jason Hervey was hired, Richard seldom went anywhere without him. Among HealthSouth employees Hervey was quietly referred to as "Mini-Me." On a trip to Boston in 2001, Richard made a presentation to a room full of analysts. Although the group was polite, Richard wasn't met with the same level of enthusiasm that he once enjoyed. The investment community had heard enough of his promises-- they wanted results. And although the company's reported earnings always came in as expected, there were enough unanswered questions and trends that always left the analysts edgy. On this particular trip, Scrushy, Hervey and Weston were flying home on the G5 jet when Hervey told Scrushy that the investor presentation "lacked sex appeal."

While still on the plane, Hervey and Richard opened the PowerPoint presentation on a laptop, and went through it, slide by slide. Hervey pointed repeatedly to how all the numbers and trends were boring. "We need something to jazz it up!" he insisted. Richard agreed wholeheartedly. He replied, "Hervey, when we get back to Birmingham, I want you to add some sex appeal to this thing. Give me music. Give me fireworks! Make it sexy!" Hervey salivated at the idea of making a contribution to an investor slide show. After all, accountants are so boring!

Hervey went to work, and two weeks later they were on the road again with a new presentation. It had everything that Scrushy and Hervey wanted--fireworks between screens, lots of his girl-band and boy-band music, and pictures of sweaty, scantily-clothed women. At the investor presentation, Weston made a point of keeping an eye on the crowd. They were numb with disbelief. Jaws dropped, heads shook, and foreheads were squeezed. The loudest noise from the room was the sound of Blackberries clicking as analysts told their offices to, "Sell, sell, sell!" Richard gave weak answers to the follow-up questions because he was truly consumed with his bands. Everything else was secondary. Afterwards an analyst pointedly asked Bill Owens, "What the hell was that presentation about?" Owens smiled, and smugly replied, "The bands keep Richard busy. You can talk to *me* about the company."

Richard, Hervey, Weston, Owens and others frequently flew to New York to meet with analysts and rating agencies. Anyone who's met with a rating agency appreciates what a grueling task that is. On a trip in 2001, Richard, Hervey, Tadd McVay (one time CFO), Bill Owens and Weston flew to New York on the Gulfstream V. Upon arrival, Scrushy and Hervey left in a limo for their own, undisclosed meeting. Bill, Tadd and Weston went to the scheduled investor and rating agency meetings.

HealthSouth stock was down at the time, and everyone they met with had hard questions on what was going on with the company. All of HealthSouth's financial indicators were showing negative trends, and for good reason; the company was in dire straits and the financials were rife with fraud. It was an extremely long day, and no one they met was remotely satisfied with their answers. At the end of the day, they all joined at the heliport in Manhattan for the short flight to Teterboro, since Scrushy and Owens had a penchant for spending thousands on a helicopter flight versus having to spend their valuable time in traffic. When Scrushy and Hervey finally showed, their arms were full of complimentary *Sony* merchandise. While Weston, Owens and McVay spent the day continually lying to Wall Street analysts, Richard and Hervey were schmoozing with Sony executives over Scrushy's crazed *Third Faze* ventures.

Richard always had to have a buddy shadowing him. His first pal, whom we'll refer to as Pal #1, was a former *Wendy's* fast food restaurant manager whom Richard met in his Sunday school class. Richard hired him and he quickly rose through the ranks in the Outpatient Rehab Division. Richard took him everywhere, including ski trips. Everyone had to treat the guy with kid gloves, because he had Richard's ear, and Richard was quick to reward or punish employees based on gossip. Richard inevitably grew tired of Pal #1 and hired Pal #2 to hang out with him. Pal #2 was better looking, had more charisma, and an attractive wife. Pal #1 was furiously jealous of Pal #2, and would trash Pal #2 every time he had the chance. Pal #2 quickly became the paid-for friend who went everywhere with Richard. However, after a couple of years, Pal #2 burned enough bridges and made enough mistakes to where Richard finally had to get rid of him like he had Pal #1. Pal #1 felt that he had a new life with Richard and was invigorated, until Richard found the pal of his dreams, Jason Hervey.

Hervey became Richard's biggest pal ever, as the two were nearly inseparable. The association became so outrageous that Richard bought radio time on a Birmingham station and the two began co-hosting an evening program. Scrushy's on-air personality was "Cowboy" and Hervey's was "Gator." They would talk on the air about Richard's toys and hobbies, and whatever else came to mind. Many, many people in the company began to believe that Richard was losing his mind.

According to Weston, Hervey was a funny guy, but he didn't have a lick of business sense. In presenting his annual budget to the assistant controller, he only completed three quarters. When she asked why, he said that he thought there were, "only three quarters in a year." What made him particularly dangerous though, was that he had Richard's ear. Seemingly, the more problems and complications the company faced, the more Richard ran to Hervey for refuge. They could talk about music, entertainment, concerts, or sexy new marketing gimmicks for days on end. The controllers couldn't keep Richard focused on anything real because he was too busy having fun with Hervey. Weston said that one of HealthSouth's attorneys once told him that he couldn't get a decision from Richard on something important because he "couldn't get Hervey out of Richard's ass long enough to ask him."

Apparently one good thing about Hervey's presence was his introduction of casual attire into the workplace. The company had previously enjoyed casual Fridays, but Hervey convinced Richard that wearing a coat and tie was old fashioned, and that as "The Healthcare Company of the 21st Century" they needed to "dress the part." In typical fashion, Richard wasn't going to do anything without some sort of promotion. He arranged for a local department store, *Parisians*, to put on a fashion show for HealthSouth employees. They set up a runway in the conference center, and all the officers were expected to take two hours out of their day to watch emaciated women and gay men prance around in the latest fashions. Richard loved the new look. It was his way of thumbing his nose at the business community and saying that he could do whatever he wanted.

Richard was also a board member of The University of Alabama. He attended a Crimson Tide Board meeting in his new casual attire. He later bragged to Weston after one of the Alabama Board meetings how those "old fogies down there needed to get with the times." However, the casual attire did not stop with the clothing. It suddenly became vogue with him and Hervey to come to work unshaven for several days in a row. Again, it fit the image of a man who was doing--and was going to do—all that he wanted.

Scrushy and Hervey's interest in the music industry became so pronounced that they apparently once worked on plans to move the accountants out of the building and convert an entire floor of the northern wing to a recording studio. I am sure the musicians would have been a lot more fun for them than the boring accountants.

Weston corroborated that during the last five years of Richard's reign he became more and more consumed with his own promotion and less and less with the improvement of the company. The highlight of his narcissism had to be in 2002 when he and Hervey rolled out the audacious "Meet the Chairman program." The party line was that with the success of the company, and its accompanying wide reach across the country, Richard could not possibly meet all the people in the field who needed to see him and who could benefit from his vast knowledge. With this program, an entire HealthSouth market could be flown in to the corporate office for a day of show and tell with The King. It was sold as a day of interaction, where these people could have an open dialogue with Richard. These thoughts could then be shared by Richard to educate other company regions on what was working throughout the country. It was also an opportunity for Richard to tell these folks just how important it was for them to "pull the wagon."

The concept of "Meet the Chairman" was actually not that bad. The thought of people being able to tell Richard exactly what their challenges were was sound. In practice though, the program turned in to another grandiose waste of money to fuel Richard's insatiable ego. A corporate jet was sent to the selected region, and along with it, a camera crew. The selected employees were filmed and interviewed with riveting questions like "Are you excited about flying on a corporate jet? How do you feel about flying to Birmingham, Alabama to meet the Chairman of the Board? Are you nervous?" The filming crews drove from the airport to HealthSouth headquarters in shiny black Suburbans, looking suspiciously like a Presidential motorcade. All of this footage and thoughtful interviewing was then converted by Hervey and the company communications department into something resembling a really bad reality TV show. The praise of the Chairman of the Board on these videos made the participants look like wannabe *American Idol* contestants. These video creations were shown at the annual administrator's meeting to foster Scrushy's "rock star" image.

In 2001, Weston attended his first HealthSouth Board of Director's retreat. These retreats were always held at exclusive resorts. In 2000, the retreat was in Cabo San Lucas, Mexico. In 2001, Scrushy held the retreat at *The Breakers*, an exclusive resort in ritzy Palm Beach, Florida. The meals and wine were absolutely extravagant. There was an afternoon golf outing, followed by a reception at Scrushy's nearby Palm Beach home, along with a moonlight cocktail cruise on his luxurious yacht. The company used at least four of its jets to fly in the board and company executives. One of Donald Trump's jets was at the Palm Beach airport at the same time, and Richard flippantly referred to it as "cheap," as he disembarked. No expense was spared as everything was being paid for by HealthSouth. All of this took place at the same time that company facilities were being told to cut costs and anyone else traveling on company business was forced to get by on a meager $20-per-day per diem.

One would think that the purpose of a board retreat would be for the board and company officers to strategize about the company's future. However, that was hardly the trip's focus. Each division president was given a small amount of time to present their respective division's business, but Richard hastily moved them through it, constantly interrupted, and became predictably angry about any deep questions, simply saying to the board, "That's not a problem! Don't worry about it!" They quickly found out why Richard rushed them--it was to get through the business so he could show his band videos. When the videos were done, he showed them an unconscionable second time--in case anyone missed any of the great lyrics. Richard even passed around a Mia Hamm soccer ball and first aid kit, and bantered about the merits of partnering with the popular sports celebrity for their continued HealthSouth branding efforts.

All of this occurred when the company was in serious trouble. HealthSouth was losing physicians, therapists, referral sources and patients. It had negative legislative initiatives on track that would potentially hurt the company if passed. There were lawsuits. HealthSouth had aging facilities with mold that could not be fixed because of cutbacks. Regardless, Richard insisted on a retreat that cost hundreds of thousands of dollars--and all he wanted to discuss during the business trip were his musical pipe dreams.

Weston said that Richard was always extremely sensitive about any criticism of him or HealthSouth. He apparently went to extraordinary lengths to locate and punish anyone who said anything negative about him or the company, including tracking down people through Internet chat rooms and suing them for libel. He became so incensed because of criticism on the *Yahoo Finance* chat board that he assigned a corporate office employee the task of making positive posts about the company and responding to the many negative comments under a number of fictitious names.

In reality, the Birmingham media was exceptionally kind to Richard. The local television stations treated him with utmost respect, and only rarely would *The Birmingham News* have anything negative to say. Richard became so upset about the few negative articles in the *News* that he eventually began encouraging employees to boycott it. His dislike for them became so pronounced that he once considered printing his own paper to compete with the local paper. He said that his paper would have good news and would promote the business community instead of "tearing it down." His vision was to use the HealthSouth print shop to produce the paper, and have prominent radio show host and columnist Paul Finebaum as the noted contributing editor. Nevertheless, the in-house newspaper never came to fruition.

Frustrated with the "lack of respect" that he was getting in Birmingham, Richard and Bill Owens even developed plans to move the HealthSouth executive offices to Palm Beach, Florida. They wanted to build a new plane hangar there replete with luxurious offices for executive level officers. Richard had a waterfront estate in Palm Beach where he spent several months of the year, and I am sure he felt much more appreciated there.

In yet a stranger twist, in late July 2002 Richard's personal accountant, William A. Massey, Jr. apparently committed suicide with a shotgun blast to the roof of his mouth after it was revealed that he was stealing money from Richard to pay for lavish meals and jewelry for his mistress, Mrs. Hope Launius. Launius was an employee at *Uppseedaisees*, the upscale pajama company financed by Scrushy to keep his third wife, Leslie, busy. According to Jim Goodreau, Richard's personal bodyguard and assistant, in a related 2003 *Birmingham News* article, Launius, with Massey's help, allegedly even paid her personal credit card bills with HealthSouth money. According to news reports, Richard discovered the marital and financial deceit by the 37-year-old Massey at least a week before his body was found on a dirt road in the back of his posh Birmingham neighborhood. Launius, like Massey, was married. Furious with Launius's transgressions, Richard made repeated calls to Mr. Launius to inform him of his wife's infidelities. The two Launiuses quickly divorced. Goodreau, a former state trooper and Montgomery policeman, claimed his job as HealthSouth bodyguard and strongman sometimes entailed other responsibilities, such as "screening mail, tracking down negative Internet message board posters and protecting HealthSouth from disgruntled spouses."

10

Weston Calls the FBI

"You Can't Just Walk Away"

Author's Note: *As stated, the story material chronicling what happened from late 1997 when I left the company to March 2003, when the fraud was revealed, was provided by former HealthSouth CFO Weston Smith. I have presented it as it was told to me by Weston. However, the following material is depicted in the first person, just as Weston wrote it. I have decided to insert it in this point of view so as to not detract from its emotional impact for the reader.*

By 2002, the level of fraud at the company was staggering. Nearly every item on the company's financial statements was laced with bogus entries. At the same time, our facilities' actual results were worsening. Competitors in many of our markets were tapping in to our patient referral sources, and many physicians began their own physical therapy operations in their own locations, eliminating those referral streams. Yet Richard was not willing to accept backing off of the earnings that would be reported since he knew it would disappoint Wall Street.

Meanwhile, legislative and regulatory issues were emerging in Washington that would have serious impacts on the company. The first of these was the Sarbanes-Oxley legislation that passed in July 2002. This legislation was a reaction to the meltdowns of Enron and WorldCom, and was intended to create strict new reporting requirements, and to increase punishment of individuals and companies who were cooking their books.

As part of Sarbanes-Oxley, HealthSouth's CEO and CFO would now be required to personally certify the veracity of the company's financial statements.

At about the same time, on another Washington front, the reimbursement by Medicare of physical therapy services was set to change. This change was released by Medicare in Transmittal 1753. The intent of 1753 was to clarify how therapy should be paid for when therapists are treating more than one patient at a time. HealthSouth therapists would routinely see more than one patient at a time, as they could see a second or third patient while the first patient was performing assigned exercises. Under 1753, many of these services would now have to be billed as group therapy, as opposed to individual therapy, which would result in a serious decrease in revenue to the company.

On July 11, 2002, Bill Owens and I told Scrushy of Transmittal 1753, and its potential to negatively impact earnings. In light of the fact that the company was already seriously overstating its earnings, I felt that it was important for Scrushy to understand that this Medicare change would be another blow to the company's earnings potential, and that our earnings should be decreased with our analysts to absorb this additional hit.

Bill and I told Richard about 1753 in the executive dining room after lunch. I conservatively estimated the impact on the company to be approximately $25 million per year. Richard listened to what we had to say, but immediately began challenging us. After articulating what the potential impact of the transmittal was, and rehashing how we couldn't absorb this kind of hit in light of the earnings overstatements that were already taking place, Richard hit the roof. His words were "Are you guys crazy? I guess you guys want to use this to cover up our other problems? We can't take the number down! If we do this, our dicks will be in the dirt forever!" He was completely incensed. He told us to "get the hell out of his way" and not to "bother him with this bullshit again."

I discovered within the week why Richard was so enraged with our news. He was quietly working with the board of directors to unload stock options of $100 million. In fact, Richard was working with the board to not only unload his shares, but to sell them at a $4 premium over what they were at on the open market! In his view, the shares were undervalued, and he felt he deserved a premium price for his many contributions to the Street. He was restricted on when he could sell stock, and alleged that he should be paid a premium price because it wasn't his fault that the stock had recently declined.   Any bad news by the company would have triggered a precipitous fall in the stock price and cost him millions. Richard eventually sold the stock at Street value, and when the news of Transmittal 1753 was eventually released, he claimed that he had no knowledge of it when he sold his stock.

Richard's reaction in the dining room that day was particularly disturbing. My reaction was that not only would Richard not accept the ongoing earnings problems, but now we had an entirely new problem that he refused to confront. I felt that there was no end in sight for the fraud. Everything about the company was fantasy, and we were now facing an entirely new challenge in Sarbanes-Oxley that Richard would not acknowledge.

At this time I learned that as CFO of the company I would be required under the new Sarbanes-Oxley legislation to sign certification documents attesting to the truthfulness of the company's financial statements. The penalty for a fraudulent certification was monetary penalties and up to 20 years in prison. Saying that this spooked me would be an understatement. On July 12th, I told Bill Owens that I would not sign the certification statement, and if necessary, would resign before doing so. I knew that I was already potentially facing serious consequences for participating in the fraud, and I had simply had enough. The certification letter was a new line in the sand that I simply did not want to cross. Enough was enough. Bill listened and would only comment on how he and Richard were committed to fixing things. He said that I was stressed because I was getting married in a week, and that I just needed the time off to charge my batteries. These discussions went on for the next week until I left for my wedding trip.

When I returned to work on the first week of August, I immediately told Bill that I had no intentions of signing the certification statement. He became angry and began playing the guilt card on me. He said that if I didn't sign the documents, I was simply going to "fuck everything up for everybody." He reminded me that I had been involved in the fraud, and that I simply could not run from my problems. Richard had earlier made it clear that "We all rode in together in this pickup truck and we are all going to ride out in it." I was seriously concerned.

I had a good relationship with HealthSouth's in-house attorney, so I talked to him about my desire to not sign the certification. We more or less talked in code, referring to "problems" at the company versus outright fraud. Just to cover himself, he said that he was talking to me as a friend, but not as a lawyer, as his professional responsibilities lay with the company. I told him of my desire to resign. After a lengthy, and in-part emotional discussion, his final reply was, "Weston, being a CFO of a publicly traded company is kind of like being a member of the mafia, you can't just walk away." I left the meeting confused, upset, angry and afraid.

The deadline for the certification statement was August 15, 2002. I continued telling Bill Owens of my reluctance to sign the statements. Finally, on August 5th, he became downright hostile about the entire matter. His exact words were that "the only excuse for a CFO to not sign the statements would be their death." Owens left my office, and I had a decision to make. Should I go along, and sign the statements, or resign and deal with whatever fallout my resignation would cause? I chose the latter. I stuffed the few personal items that I had into my briefcase and left.

I left the office and drove east on Highway 280. I was extremely upset. My new wife, also a HealthSouth employee, knew everything that was going on, so I called her and told her that I had left. We agreed to meet in the parking lot of the *Marriott* across the street from HealthSouth. After calling her, I called Owens and told him that I had left for good. He was shocked and asked what I meant. I told him that I'd quit and left the building. He was highly agitated and said that I had "another thing coming" if I thought I could just walk away.

I met my wife at the *Marriott* and was giving her a synopsis of what happened, when Owens called my cell phone. He said that he'd called Scrushy at his home office, and that the three of us must meet immediately. He said that Scrushy said he needed to do "whatever it took to get me back on the reservation." I saw no reason to meet with Scrushy after my recent "dicks in the dirt" meeting with him, but I told Owens that we could talk.

Owens came to the *Marriott*, and wanted me to get into his car. I would not because I was sure that he would only drive me to Scrushy's house. He got into my car and the three of us went for a long ride up and down Interstate 459. Owens and I had been friends for a long time. He used our past to reach out to my emotional side. We had met 20 years before at *Ernst & Young* and had many personal ties. We had seen our children born, we had taught each other to play golf, and in the past had been close friends. Over the past year, however, I had begun to seriously dislike Bill for always trying to act and think like Richard did. But on this day, Bill was just his good old self again, and he reached out to me. He spoke of the many friends we had at HealthSouth and their children, and how this whole thing would blow up if I didn't come back and sign the statements. All I knew was that I was sick of the lies, and could not stomach the thought of going back to the company and continuing the insanity.

After over two hours of this, Bill presented a new plan that he said he and Richard had created. It went like this: I would come back and sign the certification letter. In exchange, I would subsequently become CFO of the surgery center company, which would be spun off of HealthSouth. The surgery centers, because of their physician partnerships, were always kept clean and void of the fraud that was taking place. They would continue to be run properly, so I would be safe. Further, I would never have to sign another document for HealthSouth again, and I would never have to deal with the auditors. The earnings expectations in the remaining HealthSouth business would then be brought down by blaming a decline in business on

Transmittal 1753. I was promised that in the third quarter we would report what we actually generated, and that the big decline in business would be blamed on 1753. The remaining HealthSouth companies would be privatized in a leveraged buyout at their soon-to-be-diminished market value.

As a private company, Bill and Richard felt that they could clean up the financials and take the company public again in the future. In Owens' and Scrushy's mind, the shareholders would be made whole by unleashing the value of the surgery center company to them, while ridding them of a poorly performing rehabilitation company. Owens said, "We've driven our ball into the woods, but there is a gap in the trees and we can hit the green with a five iron." As preposterous as all this was, it was still a possible solution to the company's mess, and I agreed to talk to Scrushy the next day about it.

The next day, like a fool, I returned to the office to talk. Richard could turn his charm on in an instant, and that particular day was no exception. The two of us had never liked each other, but when we met he was warm and endearing, and treated me as though I were the confused child who'd run away from home, but needed to come back. Richard spoke of how we all had problems, but how running away from them wouldn't solve anything. Richard explained that as part of the new plan, he would become CEO of the surgery center company, and as his CFO we would report real earnings at the new company. He said "we're not going to let the Street tell us what we're going to do. If we have bad numbers, we'll report them." His analogy was that our earnings may be like a roller coaster, but that was alright because we were going to run it honestly. He also brought out that Owens would become CEO of the old company, and reiterated the scheme to blame the old HealthSouth's problems on 1753. I knew what I was about to do was wrong, but out of fear, guilt and worry of bodily harm, I agreed with Richard to stay on board. "So you'll sign the certifications?" Richard asked. In one of the stupidest moments of my life, I said, "Yes."

In order for the company to be able to document the "reality" of 1753 on its business, a team of HealthSouth executives flew to Washington on August 15, 2002 to meet with the Centers for Medicare & Medicaid Services (CMS) in order to "validate" that Transmittal 1753 would apply to HealthSouth. The company representatives had to of course, make an argument *against* the adoption of 1753. At one point, they were so effective in their arguments that the executive in charge of the trip had to quietly remind her associates to be careful. "We don't need to win this argument," she said.

On August 27th, 2002, the company issued a press release, citing Transmittal 1753, the split of the company, and the change in executive management. The effect of 1753, which we had originally estimated to be at $25 million, was released to the Street as a $175 million problem. The news shocked Wall Street, and our stock cratered 58 percent immediately, to just $5 per share. For that one day, despite the stock implosion, Richard remained somewhat upbeat. I believe it was because he felt that he had an escape plan for all the fraud. As CEO of the new surgery company, he could wash his hands of the old business and start something new. The rehabilitation company had an excuse for its dismal earnings, he had already unloaded millions in stock, and he had an out. On August 27, investors lost hundreds of millions of dollars in investments, but he was gleeful when we left the building. He smiled and said "I don't care if the stock hits $4 a share; we're going to get through this." I wanted to throw up.

Of course, Richard claimed he did not know of the policy change before his massive stock sale. It was a defense strategy he employed early and often as his empire was increasingly threatened. The HealthSouth Board of Directors unanimously acted to quickly remove him as CEO. This was a premeditated move by Richard to deflect the criticism by letting Bill Owens take the heat while it gave the appearance that the company was sorting out its many problems. In reality, Richard was going to work every day just as before.

Within days, the first of many shareholder lawsuits hit our desks. Shortly afterward, the SEC announced that they would begin an insider trading investigation of Scrushy's multimillion dollar stock sale made in July. Seething with anger and fear from the class action and SEC suits, Scrushy began trying to unwind the damage from 1753. The Street simply didn't believe our excuse. Other rehabilitation companies reported that Transmittal 1753 wasn't even on their radar screen. The stock continued to slide.

Richard's response was to hire a Houston law firm, Fulbright & Jaworski, who in turn hired a forensic audit group, whose job was to prove the authenticity of 1753, and more importantly to Richard--prove that he didn't know anything when he made his stock sale. In the meantime, HealthSouth's bondholders were upset with being stuck with a toxic rehab company, while the crown jewel, the surgery center division, was being spun off. More lawsuits ensued. The audit firm came in and did an exhaustive review of 1753, and similar to the results of the company's annual audits, all their questions were satisfactorily answered.

The auditors completed the lion's share of their work prior to the third quarter earnings release. Consistent with Owens' and Scrushy's promises made in July, the 3rd Quarters numbers were dramatically reduced, as they were issued with the intention of reporting "real" numbers. However, the financial results and underlying statistical data weren't even close to the information that the forensic auditors had relied upon. Within 48 hours of the earnings release, we received pages of pointed questions comparing the information that we had previously given them to what was now being reported to the Street. The questions simply could not be answered. Owens reported this to Scrushy, who immediately fired the firms from the engagement without explanation, only telling them that they "were done."

As the stock continued to slide and the lawsuits continued to mount, Scrushy began to distance himself from the entire blame game of 1753. He began saying that perhaps this rule didn't apply after all. The spinoff plan of the surgery center division collapsed in November, and Richard, through a vote of his puppets on the board, once again formally became

CEO of HealthSouth. It was a job, which in reality, he'd never quit, despite the determination of the board. Once again, formally in charge, Richard tried in earnest to do whatever it took to restore HealthSouth's image with Wall Street. Transmittal 1753 was forgotten and Owens was blamed for the company's demise. Wall Street, however, did not listen. They had been burned too many times by Richard, and nothing he said from this point forward was taken seriously.

The drumbeats started again. Scrushy was determined to restore the company's stock price, and more importantly, to rehabilitate his own name–which had taken an enormous whipping. The promises of reporting honest numbers went out the window. King Richard was back in charge full force.

I was sick of the lies, the greed, the manipulation and the never-ending manifesto of initiatives to restore Scrushy's name. There wasn't any legitimate work taking place in the executive offices. It became a mad fire drill to deal with the lawsuits, angry investors, and Richard's out of control ego. Although publicly vocal, he became somewhat more reticent behind closed doors.

In a rare glimpse of his true feelings, one day while looking out the window of the executive dining room at the digital hospital construction nearby, he whispered, "I hope I'm here to see it open." His eyes twitched at his open admission, and he angrily left the room. It was a rare view of honesty, and was quickly replaced by his new demands to once again do whatever it took to gain favor with Wall Street. After everything that I'd gone through, I could not sit back and watch the lie machine restart. I was thoroughly disgusted with Richard Scrushy and what he selfishly expected of everyone. I decided it was finally time for it to end.

I fully contemplated what a waste the past 13 years of my life had been. In order to climb the corporate ladder I had committed securities fraud, lost a good marriage, entered a bad one, and despite having become rich with the things of this Earth, felt guilty of how I'd gotten there and ashamed that I'd allowed myself to go along with the demands of a narcissist sociopath for so many years. It was time for all this to end, and whatever my punishment would be--I'd learn to deal with it. It was time to do the right thing, and to focus every new day on doing the *next* right thing.

A meeting was arranged with the FBI and the United States Attorney's office. They were familiar with Scrushy's power and greed, and felt the safest place to meet would be in the Wynfrey Hotel at the Riverchase Galleria. I was told to park my car at the opposite end of the Galleria and to take a serpentine route through the mall. I was legitimately afraid of what would happen if Scrushy knew what I was doing, and believed in my heart that he would have no boundaries in stopping me if he knew that I was about to destroy his empire. I feared for my life.

Per my instructions, I went to room 412 of the Wynfrey Hotel, and knocked on the door. When it opened, I asked for "Tom Glavine." In the room were several U.S. attorneys and FBI agents. Over the next few hours, without any promises of immunity, I laid out the true HealthSouth for them. They had no idea that such a massive fraud was occurring at the company. HealthSouth had been highly regarded within the community for years, and I was told that up to that point their only real interest was in Scrushy's suspicious stock sale.

As the case developed over the next two weeks, I subsequently met Federal officials at the *Hampton Inn* in Pell City. They did not want to meet in Birmingham for fear of us all being seen together. This meeting included the FBI, the U.S. Attorney's office, the SEC and the IRS. Frightening as it was, I had comfort that for the first time in years I was speaking the truth.

On March 19, 2003, I entered a plea agreement for my part in the HealthSouth fraud. The night before, I was in my attorney's office watching the breaking news of the FBI's raid on the corporate offices. Camera crews had set up in front of the building and beamed live broadcasts of agents sweeping through the place. It was all so surreal. The next morning, my arraignment wasn't until 10:00, and the U.S.

Attorneys' office had not yet released my name. Per their instructions, I got up and went to work as though nothing had happened, and acted as normally as any CFO of a Fortune 500 company would act the morning following an FBI raid. I left the building at 9:30 a.m., and on my drive downtown the radio news broadcasted my pending arraignment. Ironically, it was the same day that the United States invaded Iraq.

A few days later Bill Owens, acting CFO of HealthSouth, pleaded guilty to fraud and the HealthSouth Board of Directors again fired Richard—this time, for good. On April 8 Mike Martin became the ninth company official charged with fraud.

In late May acting HealthSouth CEO Robert May confirmed that Richard would never return to lead the company. The remaining HealthSouth employees cheered loudly and applauded. A *USA Today* Money article clearly depicted the grave concern among the ranks of Scrushy's return. "People at HealthSouth shudder at the prospect of Scrushy's return," said Bryan Marsal of Alvarez & Marsal, the turnaround team that was pegged to manage HealthSouth in the wake of the fraud. "It's like Freddy Kruger in Nightmare on Elm Street."

A few months after a failed, half-hearted attempt to buy HealthSouth with financing from his wealthy legal counsel, Donald Watkins, in November 2003 Richard was indicted on 85 fraud counts. His charges included wire fraud, money laundering, conspiracy and making false statements. Moreover, Assistant Attorney General Chris Wray formally charged Richard with cooking the books, making him the first CEO charged under the Sarbanes-Oxley Act. The Feds moved immediately to confiscate $278 million of Richard's immovable assets, including his many homes, which they considered ill-gotten gains. The judge set bail at $10 million, ordered him to relinquish his passport and made him wear an electronic ankle bracelet that monitored his every move. After the indictments Richard said he knew nothing of the fraud, adding that "he had no reason to destroy a company that he built and loved."

Within months of the fraud's revelation, Richard's name was removed from many of the public buildings and parkways they once graced. Profanity-laden graffiti invoking Richard's name and character appeared throughout town. The word "Thief" was even spray-painted on the bronze statue of Richard outside the Alabama Sports Hall of Fame. It was the beginning of the end of the Scrushy era in Birmingham, and a sure sign that an impending legal battle loomed large for the involved HealthSouth community.

11

The Trial

"You are a Liar!"

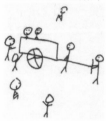

As 2003 rolled in I kept myself busy landscaping the property. With the house completed I could really see what I wanted to add in the way of plants and gardens. I was surprised at how much work it is to keep 25 acres looking good. The mowing of the grass was a full two and a half day job, not including the football field. Many times I asked myself, "Why the hell did you buy such a large amount of property?" The truth is I much enjoyed trying to make the place a showpiece, and the physical work was good for my mind and body. I can say without reservation that I slept better during those days than I ever did during my tenure at HealthSouth.

This of course all came to a quick end in March 2003 when the fraud finally broke. My attorney, Donald Briskman, and I rode together on the first of what were several trips to Birmingham. It was time well spent because it gave us a chance to get to know each other. He explained to me that once I pleaded guilty that for all practical purposes I would be a felon. I could no longer vote or own a firearm. I have never owned a gun so that was not a big deal. Losing the basic right to vote was a little unsettling, but understanding that I would carry the felon label for the rest of my life was harsh.

When we arrived at the Federal building Donald went into the meeting first, without me. When he emerged he told me that the statute of limitations for securities fraud had elapsed. He explained that I would not be charged with securities fraud. However, the statute of limitations for bank fraud is ten years. I was told I would be charged with bank fraud because I provided the banks with documents that contained fraudulent financial statements.

The meeting began with an attorney from Alice Martin's office introducing me to the others in the room. In attendance were Gerald Kelly, a special agent with the Federal Bureau of Investigations (FBI), two agents from the Securities and Exchange Commission (SEC), and two attorneys from Alice Martin's office. Alice Martin was not present. They told me that they might tape the interview. They also stressed the importance of the truthfulness and accuracy of my statements. We sat and talked for several stressful hours. Gerald Kelly, a rather large man about 6-3, 230 pounds, asked most of the questions. The fact that he was an FBI agent scared the hell out of me. I kept thinking of where I was and what a mess my life had become.

The most difficult part was that I was trying to recall events that happened six years in the past. At times they would provide facts related to some event and ask me what I remembered about it. Many times I just could not remember. I felt I was not doing a satisfactory job. They brought up the term "family" and asked me what I knew about it. I had never heard of the term, nor had I ever heard of its use at HealthSouth. They explained that it was the term often used by the people who had perpetuated the fraud. I assured them that the term must have been coined after I left the company. The SEC men asked few questions. Gerald Kelly dominated the meeting. As expected, many questions were asked about who knew about the fraud. I answered as best as I could, but I was reluctant to name people I thought might know. I was unsure how much certain people actually knew, since there was no way for me to really know if they knew or not, because I had of course never spoken to them about it. As stated, Bill Owens had politely shielded me from much of the sordid details.

The fraud began in the middle of 1996 and I was gone just after the middle of 1997. I was asked many questions dealing with points in time after I had left—questions that I could not answer. I don't believe they had a good understanding of the time line at this early stage of their investigation.

At the end of the day Gerald Kelly made me feel a little better. He thanked me for being helpful and truthful. He said he believed, from what he had already learned about the fraud, that I had told the truth. I must admit that Briskman's advice to "Tell the truth from this point forward" kept coming to mind as I was enduring questioning.

After questioning it was explained to me that I would be asked to serve as a witness at Richard's trial. It was explained that for my cooperation and truthfulness the government would take it into consideration during sentencing. However, they made clear the point that they were not "cutting me a deal." They only said that my cooperation would be favorably considered.

After returning to Fairhope within a few days I received a phone call from a Montgomery attorney. He said he was working with Richard Scrushy on the HealthSouth case and that he would very much like to meet with me to discuss the case. I told him I would check with my lawyer and get back to him. When I told Donald Briskman about the call he of course said I should not talk to Richard's lawyer. The call from the Montgomery lawyer made me uneasy. I even wondered if my phone might be tapped. I have often wondered what the motivation of the lawyer might have been. Several months later I was told through a friend that Donald Watkins, one of Richard's attorneys, wanted me to give him a call. He told my friend that he thought he could help me. I have no reason not to believe my friend, but I never called Donald Watkins.

On April 26, 2003 the headline on the front page of the *Birmingham News* read, "HealthSouth Co-Founder to Admit to Bank Fraud." This was the first time the general public was told about my part in the crime. It was another day of complete humiliation. The paper in Mobile, Alabama also ran the story, along with the *New York Times* and the *Wall Street Journal* and other newspapers across the country. The article included a picture of me and told about my position at HealthSouth and strangely, even detailed my involvement in the crawfish boil. It pointed out that the bank fraud charge carried a maximum sentence of 30 years in prison and a fine of up to $1 million. Rick Swagler, a spokesman for AmSouth Bank said that the bank was no longer doing business with HealthSouth and had lost no money because of the fraud. This was good news because I would have been liable for any money the bank had lost due to my fraud. I had always banked with AmSouth and was carrying a $600,000 mortgage with AmSouth on Beam Acres. I worried somewhat that they might call my mortgage and ask me to close my checking account. My fears did not materialize. I still bank with AmSouth today.

On May 6, 2003 in Birmingham I officially pleaded guilty to bank fraud before U.S. District Judge Robert Propst. The Judge set sentencing for July 31st. United States attorney Alice Martin said that securing guilty pleas from all five former CFO's helped to create a clear picture of the scope of the fraud.

At this time Richard had not been charged with a crime. However, the government had frozen his assets. I was now officially on record saying that Richard was the center of the fraud. I was now also officially a felon, and was again the headline story in the *Birmingham News*. I was so well-known in Birmingham I felt that it would be a relief just to get back to Fairhope where I was not such a household name. I remember buying the *Birmingham News* the morning after my pleading. As I put the paper on the convenience store counter the clerk looked at the front page of the paper and stared surprised at me. This is not the way you want to be recognized.

Back in Fairhope I was amazed at how nicely people treated me. The day after making the headlines my neighbor brought me a homemade cake and told me she and her husband were thinking of me and wished me the best. That weekend Phyllis and I went to Lulu's for breakfast. As we walked in about 20 of our friends stood up and applauded. Phyllis and I both fought off tears. I could not have asked for them to be more understanding. I had many call me and wish me the best. Also, I never received any disturbing calls from HealthSouth stockholders who lost money.

While I was in the news often, it was nothing compared to Richard. Since he denied everything his story made much better copy. At this time, in a somewhat controversial move, Richard and his wife began hosting a daily half-hour morning religious TV talk show called *Viewpoint* that catered to Birmingham's black community by entertaining as guests a regular rotation of prominent African-American preachers. It was deemed controversial by some because after the fraud broke Richard left his evangelical church in Vestavia Hills and joined a predominantly black congregation, The Guiding Light Church, in a blue-collar neighborhood. Cynical speculation suggested that Richard and his legal team were using religion to influence the jury pool.

In a February 17, 2005 *New York Times* article Paul Finebaum, the iconic Alabama statewide radio host, commented on Richard's sudden twist of faith. "In all my visits to the executive suite at HealthSouth, I never saw a black person there, not among the executives, the doctors or the secretaries. The first time I heard religion and Richard Scrushy mentioned in the same sentence was when I read about him going to the Guiding Light Church. I think he must be running out of options," said Finebaum, who once listed HealthSouth among many premier sponsors on his popular daily talk show.

Casting further doubt on the veracity of Richard's piety was that Weston Smith said that he heard from a friend and HealthSouth co-worker that Richard's personal receptionist was on one occasion caught by Richard praying on the phone in her office with a distraught friend. Richard admonished her for the incident. "Don't be praying on my time!" he ordered.

Once I plead guilty the next step was for the government to conduct a pre-sentencing investigation concerning my finances. I was due to be sentenced July 31, 2003 but we all knew I would not actually be sentenced until Richard's trial was over. For the financial investigation I had to list all of my assets and liabilities and disclose all sources of income. HealthSouth had stopped my retirement salary and all of my benefits. Phyllis was not working so our income was little. Phyllis soon took a job as a receptionist at the Catholic Social Services in Robertsdale, Alabama. She was shortly thereafter promoted to the position of office manager when the previous manager retired. The pay was modest but we both were able to get medical insurance through the position. I was instructed not to dispose of any major assets without getting permission from the government. I explained that I would have to start living off of my 401K and that I wanted to sell Beam Acres. I knew I was going to need cash to pay my legal bills and for whatever fines the government would impose. We put Beam Acres on the market with a listing price of $2.75 million even though I had put over $3,000,000 into the property.

In December 2004 the government began preparing me for the trial. Donald Briskman and I made a couple more trips to Birmingham to facilitate the process. The main attorney for the government was Richard Smith. Mr. Smith was acting head of the Justice Department's fraud division. However, much of the time Gerald Kelly from the FBI was also in the room.

The first day in preparation was spent telling my story, detailing everything I knew about Richard, HealthSouth and the fraud. It was much like my first meeting with the government in April 2003. Both lawyers present had a three-ring, four-inch thick binder full of papers. My name was posted in large letters on the binder's front cover. They of course never allowed me to look inside the binder, but I wondered how they hell they could fill such a large book with papers just about me. It made me wonder how thick Richard's binder must be. Oddly, I thought back to my days at Johnson Cover—a binder company, and how complicated and twisted my life had become since then. In retrospect, it seemed a most unlikely foreshadowing.

As I told the story they often stopped me and indicated that I had previously, in April 2003, told the facts somewhat differently. I answered that it had been almost two years since I had first told the story, and that

April 2003 was a full seven or eight years after much of it had occurred. The lawyers understood, and I realized that it was in everyone's best interest to recall the facts as best as possible. As a result, the meeting slowly proceeded.

During a break Gerald Kelly and I made small talk. When it was time to resume he confided in me. He told me not to worry. He said that compared to some of the others involved in the fraud I was going to come out in good shape. Also, my attorney, Donald Briskman, told me that as far as he could tell, the government appeared to "like me." Later that day Richard Smith explained to me that I was an extremely important witness. He said I seemed "extremely professorial," and that he felt of all the CFO's I could best explain to the jury the accounting and business terms they would need to comprehend the fraud.

The next day Richard Smith explained that the questions he asked would be the same he was going to ask during the trial. The purpose was to make me more at ease when I finally took the stand. Richard Smith did not try to tell me how to answer the questions. He explained that it would be wrong for the government to actually "coach" me on how to testify. However, at times during the "trial runs" I could tell by the attorneys' facial expressions after I answered that they didn't really like my responses.

Many of Richard Smith's questions focused on accounting terms. I was asked to explain or define terms like assets, liabilities, public company, earnings per share, investment banker, stock analyst, etc. As the questioning continued I was asked to comment on various accounting reports that would serve as evidence at the trial.

During the lunch break I was taken to the courtroom where I would testify. I sat in the witness chair. Richard Smith pointed to different spots in the room. He explained where the defense lawyers and Richard Scrushy would be seated. Richard's seat was only about twenty feet away. Of course, the purpose of this was to familiarize me with the place so that I would be more comfortable when the trial came.

That afternoon another attorney played the role of Richard Scrushy's defense lawyer. The government warned me that Richard's lawyers would not be nice. They explained that the defense's job would be to discredit me in any way they could. Richard Smith said that my marriage, my drinking and my gambling would all be fair game once I was on the stand. Before the role-playing began I was asked to talk about these difficult issues. I was even asked if Phyllis and I ever participated in sex parties with other HealthSouth executives. I told them I was never invited to such an activity. For the rest of the afternoon I wondered who at HealthSouth had sex parties.

Going into these meetings I was confident that the government had a great case. I really could not see how they would lose. However, I did not sense great confidence among the government legal team. Much of this had to do with legal squabbles between them and my lawyer as to what the judge would allow to take place in the courtroom.

At the end of the meeting everyone thanked me and said they believed I would do a great job. I was told I would have one more preparatory meeting before the trial, which was scheduled to begin on January 5, 2005.

The day before the trial began I drove to Birmingham to spend the night with my daughter Jennifer. I normally have no trouble sleeping. I am a sound sleeper. However, that night, due to anxiousness, I only got about three hours of restless sleep. I took a short run early the next morning to help me clear my head. Jennifer drove me to meet with Donald Briskman at Richard Smith's office prior to going to court. He was already having a meeting with Richard Scrushy's lawyers and I believe the Judge, Karen O. Bowdre. Richard Scrushy's lawyers were surprised that I was to be the first witness for the prosecution. This apparently caused some sort of problem. This was the first of many disputes the lawyers had during my testimony, which caused the trial to move along at a snail's pace.

After a thirty minute delay Donald and I proceeded to the court room. I saw numerous television trucks outside the building and as we approached a beehive of reporters and camera men tried to interview me. We just kept walking and said nothing.

Security to enter the Federal building was much like what you would find at an airport. We removed our shoes and our cell phones were not allowed. There were also no cameras allowed, not even for the press. Phyllis did not want to be at the trial, or even in Birmingham. I certainly was not disappointed. Had she been there it would have likely been even more stressful.

I was extremely nervous. I felt like everyone was looking at me. I was taken to the witness waiting room. I sat there alone for some time. I discovered that I was actually not the first person to be called to testify. There were several witnesses who testified before me that had lost money in HealthSouth's stock due to the fraud. The entire morning passed without me being called. After lunch I was finally summoned. However, there was another unforeseen legal snafu which caused the judge to call for a break. I was sent back to the waiting room for another excruciating wait.

There were a few outdated magazines to read but as I tried to pass the time. I found myself reading the same sentence over and over and not comprehending any of it. I could only think about what it would be like in the courtroom.

The trial proceedings finally began with Richard Smith calling me to the stand. The court room was packed. Just as the government had told me during the prep session, Richard Scrushy was only 20 feet away from me to my left. The jury was directly across the room and Judge Bowdre was to my right. Richard's wife, Leslie, was at his side, along with several of his black supporters, who were clutching Bibles. I was nervous but my voice held steady as I began answering Richard Smith's questions. It was not that bad because it was just like the practice runs.

After several background questions Richard Smith asked me to explain various financial terms to the jury. I tried to maintain good eye contact with each jury member. Nevertheless, I saw them quickly lose interest in my testimony. I do not believe they understood much of what I explained. Richard Smith even displayed on a video screen images of actual accounting documents, so as to aid my explanation. It did little good. A few of the jurors appeared to be nodding off to sleep. The day ended without the defense taking their turn cross-examining me. Before exiting, everyone waited until the jury filed out of the opposite side of the courtroom.

Donald Briskman met me and we left the court building together. Predictably, the press again bull-rushed us once we were outside. Donald of course told me to make no comments. All my life I had seen movies and news coverage with scenes like this. I thought of how all of this was so foreign to me—being questioned by FBI agents, pleading guilty to a felony, being a key government witness in the most sensational trial in Alabama state history, and now—being mobbed by the media. Of course, none of these new experiences were aspirations of mine.

I called Jennifer and she soon drove and picked me up. I was somewhat relieved that the trial had finally begun, but I knew the worst was ahead of me. I called Phyllis and told her how the day went. The judge instructed me to not watch the news or read about the trial in the papers. Sleeping that first night was a little better. I was exhausted and my body needed rest.

The next morning Donald Briskman assured me that I had done a good job and that the lawyers for the government were pleased. The day started much like the day before with both sets of lawyers arguing before the judge about procedural matters. I was sent back to the waiting room for what seemed like hours.

Before the defense had its turn at me the judge asked that I come to her chambers with an attorney from each side. She instructed me to tell in a summarized fashion what happened. She told the lawyers they could not ask questions and that nothing was being recorded. The jury of course did not hear what I said.

I told her what happened that day in Richard's office and how the fraud continued until I left in 1997. I could tell it was killing Richard's lawyer not being able to jump in, but she just held up her hand every time he tried. At the end she told me she knew about my crawfish boils and had heard many good things about them. I found the meeting odd. I am not totally sure why she did it.

Before lunch I was again called to the stand. I began by telling the sequence of events that occurred leading to that fateful summer day in 1996. I explained how Bill Owens and I had made every aggressive accounting entry we could but that the 2nd quarter numbers were still short of Wall Street expectations. I detailed how we told Richard Scrushy that it was time to report bad numbers and how he said no, that it was not an option. I explained how Bill Owens then changed the numbers at Richard's request and how Richard approved the earnings news release knowing the books had been cooked. My remaining testimony was about repeating the fraud in future quarters and my decision to leave the company in the middle of 1997.

That afternoon the government turned me over to Richard Scrushy's legal team for cross-exam. I soon realized that Jim Parkman was extremely theatrical. He played well the role of the "Aw shucks country lawyer." It truly was like something out of a movie, and I could immediately tell that the jury was more attentive to him than they had been to Richard Smith, who like his name, was plain and not the least bit entertaining. Parkman sought to make the trial fun for the jurors.

Parkman asked me many questions about a particular accounting report that was central to the government's case against Richard. It was a weekly revenue report—one that was produced every Friday afternoon. Parkman compared actual revenues compared to budgeted revenues for every operating unit in the company. The point was made by the government that in many cases the reports showed that in total the company on a weekly basis was missing its budgeted revenues during 1996. However, the financial statements we were reporting to the world showed the company right on target with expectations. Parkman made the statement to me that "I bet you" the government had "cherry-picked" the worse weeks to prove their point. I had scrutinized these reports in great detail in my pretrial preparations and I was able to recall there were worse reports not entered as trial evidence. When he said "I bet you" I quickly said, "How much do you want to bet?" The courtroom erupted with laughter. At the day's end Bill Owens' attorney told me that in his 30 years in the courtroom he had never heard laughter so loud. However, my fun moment quickly passed as Parkman began his personal attack.

Parkman asked me if I had a girlfriend while working at HealthSouth. I quickly admitted that I did. The pretrial preparations had readied me for this, and I had even discussed it with Jennifer and Phyllis, and that it was likely to be brought out in the trial. This was a bridge that we had already crossed as a family, many years before. Phyllis and I had been married for 33 years. We were past this. Nevertheless, Parkman continued. He asserted that I had a drinking and a gambling problem while I worked at HealthSouth. I denied this. I felt that I certainly did not have a gambling problem, although I was well aware that I had probably drank too much during my days owning and managing the night clubs. Parkman mentioned that I had operated "bars" on the side, failing to mention of course that one of the bars was co-owned by Richard. I really did not want to argue my drinking habits with Parkman. I simply said that I did not have a drinking problem and left it at that.

That night my personal life was in the news. Parkman was painted as having successfully forced me to admit infidelity. To this day it makes my blood boil. After all, I was under oath! I was asked the question and had to tell the truth! It was not in the least bit clever on his part. I simply did not lie. Furthermore, it had nothing to do with the fraud!

It still angers me that Richard did not take the stand. The defendant in these cases has a great advantage in that they do not have to lie or tell the truth. They simply do not have to testify because of the Fifth Amendment to the Constitution.

When I talked to Phyllis that night she was great. She told me she was thinking about coming to Birmingham the next day. She wanted to stand outside the courthouse with a large sign that said, "Aaron and I have been married 33 years—our only marriage." Richard Scrushy, of course, was on his third marriage. A year or so after the trial I learned that Parkman was on number four. Jennifer and I did not talk about the infidelity. She simply hugged me and told me she loved me dearly.

Jennifer and Phyllis are special people. It is difficult for me to say who was hurt the most by the Wagon to Disaster. The hard part for Jennifer was that she moved to Birmingham when she was nine years old. She grew up in Birmingham and became known as the daughter of the founder of both HealthSouth and the crawfish boil. Hundreds of her friends attended the crawfish boil annually, and for a while she even managed the event. When the fraud broke in 2003 she was the maitre d at Highlands Bar & Grill, which is without question Birmingham's most public place. Chef Frank Stitt and his restaurant are known and respected throughout the United States. It is also the watering hole for all of the pretty people in Birmingham. When movie stars and other celebrities are in town, they hit the Highlands Bar & Grill. To this day I tear up when I think about her having to greet everyone coming into the restaurant during all of this. She is a brave individual. Jennifer said that most people were kind to her during the turmoil, but that it still hurt nevertheless. She said that only one person ever said an unkind word to her about my role in the fraud. She said that when the news broke regarding the fraud she was working at the Highlands in the evenings and during the day at the Hopson James Salon in Homewood. She said she was in the salon that afternoon and a woman abruptly came to her and said, "Your daddy is going to jail!" I cannot express how proud I am of my daughter. Jennifer, I love you. Thanks for standing by me. You and Phyllis have made me a better person.

After the personal attacks Parkman began questioning me about that day in 1996 when we first falsified the numbers. He tried to get me to tell the jury exactly what Richard told us to do. He asked me if Richard told us to commit fraud, with the word fraud being the operative term. He asked if it was possible that when he said "fix" the numbers that he really only wanted us to do our job as accountants. I assured him that Richard knew he was asking us to make the number match Street expectations. However, Parkman continued to question my memory. He even suggested that I had "selective memory." I finally asked him if I could say something that might help him understand. Surprisingly, he said "sure." I said, "When I was a little boy I remember getting a new bicycle for Christmas. But, if you ask me what my parents said that day and what words of thanks I used, I cannot tell you; but I damn well know I got a bike that Christmas, just like I know Richard asked me and Bill to commit fraud—regardless of whether or not he used the word fraud when he asked." This was effective in forcing him to move on to the next issue— me being a liar.

Parkman asked, "When you presented the numbers to investors in 1996 and 1997, you lied, didn't you?" He continued, "When you presented to the Board of Directors, you lied, didn't you?" By now he was really loud and he almost seemed to scream the word "lie" at the end of each question. He asserted that I had lied so much that I could not tell if I were telling the truth or another lie. The jury appeared spellbound. No one was sleeping. All 24 eyes were wide open. Finally he said, "Mr. Beam, I only have one more question and you can step down. "Did you lie to your wife?" I said yes. I was under oath.

The prosecution centered its closing arguments on depicting Richard as the one person at HealthSouth who benefited the most from the fraud. According to a *New York Times* article, lead prosecutor Alice Martin referred to Richard as "The Pied Piper," adding, "it was his company, it was his reward, and that reward was money." She also noted that Richard exercised more than $201 million in stock options over the six-year period in which HealthSouth was cooking the books. "Mr. Scrushy is the quintessential micromanager," she told the jury. "He had his finger on the pulse of HealthSouth."

The prosecution also played for the jury portions of one of the secret recordings made by Bill Owens for Federal investigators before the HealthSouth offices were raided by the government. On the tapes, prosecutors argued that Richard was trying to convince Bill not to disclose the fraud, telling him at one juncture that Richard's children "need their daddy." Alice Martin forcefully quipped, "Where did he think daddy was going to go?"

Lead defense counsel Donald Watkins used the final minutes of his rebuttal to try and establish a distinctively Southern connection between Richard and the jury. "Your job is to police the government of the United States of America," he informed them, saying their duty was to protect Richard from the harm of the U.S. Government. He finished with a status appeal, "The big shots in Washington are watching you--I'm talking about that bourbon-sipping, martini-drinking, cigar-smoking club."

12

The Verdict

"I'm Going to go to my Church and Pray"

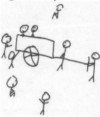

My planned participation in the trial was over. However, I was warned again by the judge not to read or listen to news about the trial. There was a small chance I could be called to testify again or there could be another trial if the jury could not reach a verdict.

That night Jennifer and I went to Ruth Chris' Steakhouse. We needed something nice to put the past few difficult days behind us. The maitre d told us that some of Richard Scrushy's legal team was staying at the hotel nearby. He said he would seat us in an out-of-the-way table so we could avoid them if they came in for their usual drinks.

Early the next morning I received a call from Donald Briskman. He told me that he did not think it was a good idea for me to "be out on the town with a young, attractive woman." I explained to him that the rumor mill failed to point out that the attractive woman was my daughter. The next day I was happy to be home in Fairhope, away from the news and innuendo.

Phyllis and I knew the trial would continue for a long time. Our future was so uncertain. My sentencing, as expected, was delayed until after Richard's trial was completed. Alice Martin's people had told Donald Briskman that they were pleased with my testimony. But at this point they would not comment on how much prison time they would recommend for me.

Before the trial began I enrolled at Faulkner State Community College and began working toward a two-year certificate in golf course and turf management. I knew I could not find a job related my past and I did not have a desire to do so; but I also knew that Phyllis and I would need more than her income from CSS. I must say I enjoyed being back in the classroom studying something that had nothing to do with business. With the turf management certificate I would be able to work at a golf course, high school or university with sports fields, city park departments, or just use what I learned in my own lawn business. I have always enjoyed gardening and working outside. Phyllis and I agreed that this was the best way for me to start a new life. I became good friends with Kent Schwartz, the coordinator of the landscape and golf management program at Faulkner State. I shared with him my situation and he of course had no problem with my past.

Meanwhile, we were getting no offers on Beam Acres. People loved to look at the place but I don't believe we saw more than one or two serious buyers while it was listed with a real estate agent. Our plan was that Beam Acres would be the last piece of property we would ever own. Thus, we did not build everything on the property for resale value. Our only hope of getting close to what we had put into it was to find a buyer who wanted a special estate complete with a regulation football field, guest house, swimming pool, catfish pond and outdoor stage.

Months passed and our future was still not coming into focus. On May 19, 2005 the government rested its case against Richard. The jury began its deliberations, trying to ascertain whether or not Richard was guilty of fraud. Over a month later, on June 28, the jury of seven men and five women reached a verdict. However, the verdict did not come easy. At one point during their lengthy deliberations the jury told the judge that they were potentially deadlocked. The judge instructed them to work towards a decision, reminding them that a hung jury would result in a retrial. A few days later, the judge replaced an ill juror. Shortly thereafter a verdict was reached.

On June 28, 2005 several friends in Birmingham called before the news broke to inform me that the jury had come to a decision and that a news conference was immediately forthcoming. Hours later the news broke. Amazingly, they found Richard Scrushy not guilty on one count of conspiracy, two counts of securities fraud, 13 counts of wire fraud, seven counts of mail fraud, two counts of making false statements, one count of false certification and ten counts of money laundering—in all, not guilty, on 36 counts.

The sight of Richard and his wife Leslie celebrating on camera outside the courthouse was more than I could handle. On the courthouse steps Richard made the following comments, "I'm going to go to my church and pray. I am going to be with my family. Thank God for this." Additionally, he thanked his "praying partners," the same ones that had flanked him in the courtroom throughout the trial. "Jesus taught us how to love each other," he said. "What has happened to the compassion in this world? We've got to have compassion, folks, because you don't know who's going to be attacked next."

I was not sure how I was going to react to a not guilty verdict but I was surprised at how much it really upset me. That afternoon I went to class at Faulkner. I was the first student in the classroom and the instructor, Kent Schwartz, arrived before any of the other students. He said he heard the news. He asked me how I was doing. I tried not to be upset but I visibly fought back tears. He deliberately walked out of the room, giving me a chance to compose myself. In retrospect, I don't believe I heard a thing he said in class that evening about soils and fertilizers.

With the trial over I was free to read the newspapers and review other news sources related to the trial. I wanted to know—along with the rest of the country—what went wrong. If it had to be summed up, the prosecution most likely failed because Richard had a home field advantage. According to an article in the *USA Today* newspaper, for white-collar prosecutions, the government fares best in New York, where prosecutors have vast experience presenting securities fraud cases, judges are well-versed in the particular area of the law and there's a much greater likelihood a jury will include someone with a financial background. The parallel convictions of Worldcom's Bernie Ebbers and Tyco's Dennis Kozlowski were secured in New York. In hindsight, trying the case in Richard's back yard of Birmingham was not a good idea, as Richard was a perceived favorite son of the community. Also, I think the prosecution—namely Alice Martin, like many others in this story, completely underestimated Richard Scrushy.

There were undoubtedly numerous other contributing factors to the prosecution's failure and the victory for the defense. Among them was the clever defense strategy of discrediting key prosecution witnesses. They used every bit of dirt on us that they could find. They dug deep into all of our personal lives. Moreover, Richard's attorneys made all of us out to be rats—lying rats, and they were undoubtedly effective at painting that ugly picture for the jurors. Defense attorney Jim Parkman even went as far as to create a large poster adorned with a gray cartoon rat to vividly prove his point. On another courtroom day Parkman even wore a tie emblazoned with rats eating cheese.

Also, some of us made better witnesses than others. In retrospect, Bill Owens was a terrible witness; and his secret recordings of Richard and himself, made from a hidden tie microphone, proved to be ineffective, and in some cases even misleading. For instance, during one section of the recordings, Richard's comments suggested he was innocent. He said, "You will never and I will never put anything on the balance sheet or on the income statement that is not 100% accurate, you agree?" I was always concerned about this particular statement and I have wondered whether Bill tipped Richard off that he was being recorded, as Richard had to at least suspect it. Then again, it could have been a complete guess on Richard's part. Of all of us Bill got the worst sentence—five years, and he is now destitute, and single, as a result, as his wife of over thirty years divorced him after the fraud broke. Nevertheless, Bill did not help the prosecution.

Richard's defense position of "not knowing about the fraud" succeeded where other high-profile CEO's like Ebbers' and Kozlowski's had failed.

This of course brought new challenges toward enforcing the Sarbanes-Oxley Act, the statute Congress passed in 2002 to compel companies to strengthen their internal controls as well as establish penalties for CEO's and CFO's who sign false financial filings.

In post-trial comments juror Christopher Cooper, a 37-year old father of five and Air Force reservist, said he simply could not believe the testimony of the government's star witness, Bill Owens, after Owens admitted that he had not paid his income taxes for nine years and had lied about a $1.3 million loan from HealthSouth.

Lutheran Harris, a 33-year old supervisor for a private security company, said the government didn't present adequate evidence for a conviction. "Of course it was proven that it was fraud at the company," said Harris, "but there was not enough evidence to prove that Mr. Scrushy was involved."

Another juror, Debra Williams, a 50-year old African-American woman, wondered why there was no physical evidence linking Scrushy to the crime. "They should have gotten fingerprints on those records," she said.

"There just wasn't enough evidence. There was reasonable doubt. There were inconsistencies that I couldn't get around. There were holes not filled for me," said Natosia Burks-Bell.

Still another juror wondered why there was no recording of Richard using the word "fraud."

It seems that jurors today have been unduly influenced by television programs like CSI (Crime Scene Investigation) that depict court cases relying heavily on forensic evidence to solve crimes. The fact that the prosecution had no physical evidence in the case was apparently troubling in the eyes of the jury. It seems that they would have indeed been better served if they had a tape where Richard actually told one of us to "commit fraud," or a doctored financial document containing his fingerprints.

Another odd fact in the case was that U.S. District Judge Karon O. Bowdre, the judge who presided over the trial, was doing so for the first time. In a case as large and far-reaching as this one was, it is strange to think that the government would tap a woefully inexperienced rookie judge to preside. Moreover, as it turned out, the prosecution had little chemistry with the judge, as she seemingly sided with the defense on many objections—including the extremely important defense tact of attacking the personal lives of former HealthSouth employees. In short, Judge Bowdre allowed the defense to run the courtroom.

Factoring largely into the outcome was the jury composition, which was majority black with seven blacks and five whites, and predominantly working-class. Furthermore, of the 18 jurors and alternates available for the trial, 11 were African-American. The defense attorneys played on this fact in their closing arguments when they emphasized Richard's upbringing in Selma, Alabama where state troopers assaulted civil rights marchers in 1965. They also noted to the jury that during that time period juries played a powerful role in reversing past racial injustices in the United States. Couple this with Richard's many generous donations to black churches and his ongoing daily TV show which he used to showcase his newfound black minister friends and a reasonable person could see where Richard had effectively laid the groundwork to make himself appear as a trusted friend of the black community in Birmingham. This was evidenced by the fact that daily in court Richard was flanked by his many recently-acquired black minister acquaintances and other high-profile members from the black community, like former Birmingham Mayor Richard Arrington.

The grand irony in this is that from the beginning Richard was successful at maintaining an unwritten HealthSouth policy of purposefully not hiring blacks. During the first decade of the thirteen years that I co-founded and worked for the company, Richard never hired a single black person. Weston Smith recalled that Bill Owens told him that Richard once said, "We're not going to hire any niggers here at HealthSouth." Furthermore, Richard's popular "pulling the wagon" mantra was paradoxically a racist, Southern plantation term often used by overbearing slave masters to increase slave production.

2003 Internal Revenue Service records indicate that Richard's charitable foundation gave the Guiding Light Church $1 million. In 2004, the foundation gave another $700,000 to various black religious organizations. Some of the leaders of these organizations made up the now-infamous "Amen Corner" that were a constant courtroom presence during the trial.

However, not all of the black Birmingham preachers were happy with Richard's generosity. In fact, some found fault with his newfound faith. One of Richard's former supporters, Pastor Herman Henderson of Believers Temple Church, alleged that Richard hired him to organize black pastors to regularly attend the trial and to provide public relations services. These alleged services included writing helpful news articles that were placed in *The Birmingham Times*, a local publication serving primarily the black community. Pastor Henderson's assistant, Audrey Lewis, admitted writing articles that were reviewed by Richard Scrushy and then submitted to the Birmingham Times for placement. Richard later acknowledged that his charitable foundation gave Henderson's church at least $15,000, but he said it was for a building project and a Hurricane Katrina relief effort.

In addition to the race factor, there was also the possibility that Southerners on the jury were distrustful of the Federal Government. Of the ten plea bargain deals cut by the Feds with key former HealthSouth executives prior to the start of Richard's trial, only one received jail time. The others were given only home detention or probation. Richard's attorneys brought this fact up repeatedly during the trial.

Waging war with the United States Government is a harrowing proposition. Most defendants—about 90 percent, lose. They lose because the government has unlimited resources and the ability to pick the venue. However, in Richard's case, he was much different from the average defendant because he spent $25 million on his own defense. Few defendants have those kinds of resources. Moreover, Richard used his resources wisely. He not only hired a team of talented attorneys, he built a website to promote his innocence, and helped his son-in-law purchase a small television station where he ran daily commentary on the trial that effectively bolstered his image as a favorite son. Furthermore, he made hefty donations for the construction of black churches and hosted his own daily TV segment in which he interviewed popular black preachers.

Despite the outcome, there were many who believed that justice was at least partially served because of the fact that Richard had to spend $25 million of his ill-gotten gains to defend himself. Few realize that he received a payment of over $17 million from HealthSouth's insurance company to reimburse him for his legal costs. Richard and I both had insurance protecting us personally from lawsuits. It is called officers' and directors' insurance and it kicks in only if you successfully defend yourself. Since Richard was successful in defending himself, he was granted the funds by the insurer. Another related fact is that much of the money given to his defense attorney Jim Parkman's firm was funneled in fees to Richard's other son-in-law, who was a partner with Parkman's law firm.

After the trial I was demoralized. The thought of Richard not having to take the stand and endure the biting criticism and interrogation associated with cross-examination that we had to was nauseating. However, realizing that Richard would not have to go to prison, that he would be repaid the bulk of his legal fees and would not have to forfeit any of his wealth and property was overwhelming. It was unfair. In my eyes, and in the eyes of many, justice simply had not been served.

I went before U.S. District Judge Robert Propst for sentencing on August 26, 2005. Donald Briskman had met with Alice Martin's staff several times to try and secure for me little or no jail time. He also negotiated the monetary fines I had to pay. He told me before I faced Judge Propst that the government was recommending a three-month prison sentence and a $275,000 forfeiture. Ultimately Judge Propst handed down the recommended sentence and monetary forfeiture plus a $10,000 fine and one year of probation.

Judge Propst said that he had no reason to doubt my trial testimony, punctuating the statement with the somewhat risqué remark, "I guess somebody out there is still looking for the real killers." The judge added during the sentencing hearing that I was "certainly not the worst fish in the sea in this deal." However, he said probation was not an option under the law because of the seriousness of the charge.

I could now in the near future add "prison time" to my resume'. A few months later Phyllis and I went to Mobile and heard the legendary Austin, Texas musician Marcia Ball perform. She was a good friend from the height of our crawfish boil days, as she had entertained us on more than one occasion. After the show that night Marcia invited us backstage. She told me that she was proud of me because "all real men in Texas drive pickup trucks, have been drunk and have spent time in prison."

The sentencing day in court was another terrible day in my life. It was trying because so many of my family and friends were there in support of me. I appreciated their presence, but it was extremely emotional having them there. When I was asked to speak it was difficult. I was able to manage a brief statement. I said that I should have stood up to Richard Scrushy and said no, but I didn't. I still think that the HealthSouth fraud may have never happened if I had said no to Richard back in 1996. I will never escape the fact that the fraud began on my watch. I have often wondered if the others that took part in the fraud might hold a grudge against me because I was the first person between Richard and the others. Bill Owens, Mike Martin and Weston Smith all got more prison time than I did. I cannot say if that is right.

The judge allowed me to remain free on bond until November 1st. Beam Acres was set to be auctioned on October 5, 2005. We had made the decision several months earlier because we had received no realistic offers through real estate agents. I had to borrow money from my sister Janice and friend Greg Browne to pay the up-front auction expenses.

Phyllis and I had depleted our cash reserves over the last two and a half years since the fraud broke and HealthSouth had stopped my retirement income. All of our net worth was in the property.

The auction day was another intense episode. Phyllis could not bring herself to be present at the auction. She went to work and told me to call her when it was over. Weeks earlier we had a huge garage sale to sell off my tractor, the football field Reel mower, my Gator utility vehicle and other items I clearly would no longer need. These were mostly my "man toys" that I hated to part with--but I had no choice.

There were roughly 15 to 20 qualified bidders at the auction for Beam Acres. I had hoped for many more. Surprisingly, there were three different auto dealers among the group. The bidding took no more than 15 minutes. Only five people took part in the actual bidding, and it really came down to only two who were serious about a purchase. The final bid was just over $2,000,000. Phyllis and I wanted more, however. At this point we had a clear indication of what our fines from the government and other financial obligations were. We needed about $1,500,000 to pay the government for fines, income taxes due from the sale of real estate prior to the fraud breaking, for the mortgage on Beam Acres, for the auction fee and outstanding credit card debts. The balance of the proceeds was available to buy a new home and begin our new life. We did not know what additional fees we owed Donald Briskman.

The auction occurred on October 5th and I was to report to prison on November 1, 2005. Phyllis had been looking for a house to buy but of course could not make an offer until the auction was completed. This was not a good time to buy a home as there were few homes for sale in the Lower Alabama area as Hurricane Katrina victims seeking a new place to live had made it a real seller's market. Phyllis found two homes she liked but did not make offers, as she wanted to fully investigate the market. She found nothing else that she liked. She went back to the two original homes, only to find them both under contract. This all happened over a matter of days.

With only two weeks before I was to report to Federal prison we found a house we both liked in Loxley, Alabama, a small town off of Alabama State Highway 59, south of Interstate 10, about 25 miles from the "T" at Gulf Shores. While the real estate agent was showing us the house she said a buyer had just made an offer but had not yet signed the papers. Phyllis pointedly asked the agent if the deal was for list price. The agent said no. Phyllis told her that we would pay full price and sign the papers as fast as they could type them. We got the house and later heard that the people who made the earlier offer were not happy.

The house was vacant so we talked the seller into renting it to us in the interim so we could begin moving. My friend Tommy Washington, the gentleman who built the football field at Beam Acres, graciously helped us with the move. He had a crew of four men and several large trucks. It was quite an ordeal to get Phyllis settled before I left. In fact, the move was not completed by the time I left for prison. Phyllis had to handle about half of it without me. I hate moving, but Phyllis suggested that I contact the sentencing judge to see if I could get my reporting date pushed back a few weeks so I could help her. Needless to say, I did not take her up on the idea, as I was ready to get it over with and I truly hate moving.

13

I'm in the Jail House Now

"The Drug Dealers From Miami"

On October 27, 2005 news agencies reported that Richard Scrushy was indicted along with former Alabama Governor Don Siegelman on bribery charges related to his coveted position on the Alabama Certificate of Need Review Board that controlled the direction and scope of the health care industry within the state. Since his June 28th acquittal, Richard had much enjoyed the redemptive limelight. He continued his television program as well as regular speaking appearances within the black community. For Richard, the show seemingly never stopped. He even proffered himself as a white collar crime expert, attending the late Enron CEO Ken Lay's trial, and was subsequently interviewed for national television where he discussed how Lay bungled his defense. In hindsight, this was likely all by design, as it was revealed on October 27th that the second indictment was returned earlier that year in May, but sealed pending jury deliberations in the securities fraud case.

The news of Richard's second indictment was welcomed, as I was headed into a three-month prison term, starting in a matter of days. Although misery certainly loves company, however, like most that understood the facts relating to the second indictment, I doubted seriously if Richard would be convicted; I simply felt that the government had missed its chance to land the big fish earlier that year in Birmingham.

On the morning of November 1, 2005 Phyllis drove me to Maxwell Air Force Base in Montgomery, Alabama. I was self-reporting. Maxwell is a minimum security Federal prison camp and many inmates self report as a result. One point of fact worth mentioning is that throughout this entire sordid ordeal I was never once handcuffed. It was a disgrace that I fortunately never experienced.

We arrived at 8:00 a.m. as directed. The Air Force guard at the gate pointed where we were to park and instructed that a bus from the base would soon be around to deliver me to the prison. It was almost two hours until the bus arrived. Another future inmate boarded the bus with me. Phyllis and I said our quick goodbyes, although I knew she would be visiting me on the weekends during my 90-day stint. The ride to the prison took several minutes. We were taken to an "intake building" to be processed.

As I reported to a prison official he checked me off of a computer-based report and instructed me to have a seat until I was called for processing. It was afternoon before they began to deal with me. I was given a rules and regulation book that I was told to read while I waited. My photo was taken and I was fingerprinted. By the way, I still have my prison identification card. I was totally disrobed and was body searched. Everything except my wedding ring, underwear and tee shirt were packaged and mailed to Phyllis. I was given a pair of green pants and a green shirt. I was happy to discover that it was not orange. They asked me my shoe size and I was issued a pair of socks and boots that were about two sizes too large. I was told I could change out the next day any items that did not fit. I was also given a set of sheets for the bed but no pillow.

The officer processing me was somewhat of a comic. He said I "looked like a fighter" but hoped I would not fight while I was there. He assured me that if I did I would be sent to "Big Boy" prison. He added that if I did not like it there "I could leave." He said, "You have probably noticed by now that there are no walls or locked gates. You can leave if you want, but the U.S. Marshals will find you and you will go to 'Big Boy' prison for a long time." He asked why I was there. I told him and he said he was aware of the HealthSouth case. He asked me if I worked for

Richard Scrushy and I said yes. He did not talk about it anymore. I believe that prison officials are discouraged from talking to inmates about their crimes.

The processing took the entire day. The time was spent mostly waiting. I was walked to the cafeteria just before it was closing. I was told to always walk on the sidewalks and to never walk on the grass. Along the way the guard pointed to the building where I would be housed. The official in charge of the building showed me my bed and reminded me that I should be in it by 10:00 p.m. for a head count. All inmates were counted five times a day—at 12:00 a.m., 3 a.m., 5:00 a.m., 4:00 p.m. and 10:00 p.m. All counts were done at bed side. The early morning counts were done while you slept. You could not miss a count. If an inmate was not accounted for the camp would be locked down until his whereabouts were explained. The count was never short while I was there.

Next to my bed I had a locker. It was about 40" by 30" by 24." I also had a metal folding chair. I was issued four green uniforms, three tee shirts, three underwear, three pair of socks, boots, a cap, a coat, sheets and three towels. It was hard to believe that after owning so many worldly things that my total possessions fit into such a tiny space.

During my first full day I was able to go to the camp store. I put $500 into my account when I was processed. We were allowed to buy $300 worth of merchandise each month from the camp store. It was called "Wal-Mart." I had wondered before reporting how I would purchase things when I was in prison. It was easy. You were not allowed to bring anything into prison. Therefore, I needed many things. For instance, I get heartburn if I don't take Prilosec daily. The Prilosec at the prison store, like most other things, was expensive. One container was $17. I soon learned that every inmate has to have a few things that were sold in the camp store. I spent $284 the first day, leaving me $16 for the remainder of the first month. My big ticket items were a pocket radio, headphones, Nike shoes, sweatpants, and basic things like a toothbrush, toothpaste, coffee mug, writing materials, a lock for my locker and some food items.

It was truly amazing how my day-to-day outlook on life changed once I was in prison. I did not save the box my shoes came in. I soon realized I needed something in my locker for small items such as writing materials, toothpaste, a toothbrush, etc. A fellow inmate told me he was getting new shoes the next day and that he would give me his empty box. I actually looked forward to getting that box. Times had certainly changed. Before prison I looked forward to getting a new car.

The lights were turned on at 5:00 a.m. each day and breakfast was available until 6:30 a.m. The work day was from 7:00 a.m. until 2:00 p.m. Lunch was from 10:30 a.m. until noon and the evening meal was served from 4:30 until 6:00. I was in prison for such a short period of time that I was not given a regular job. Instead, I had to help clean our living quarters from 7:00 a.m. until 2:00 p.m. This entailed cleaning everything we used—toilets, sinks, mirrors, floors, etc. The balance of the day was my time. There was actually not enough work to do for those assigned to clean the living space. As you might expect there are many men in prison with little meaningful work. After I cleaned what really needed to be cleaned, I just tried to look busy. For instance, I sometimes washed the same window ten times. Of course, trying to look like you are working is harder than actually working. Boredom was a real issue.

At 2:00 p.m. every day I changed into my sweat suit and running shoes for the balance of the day. I did a lot of walking while I listened to my radio. On most afternoons I listened to the Paul Finebaum sports talk show out of Birmingham. I remember one day Paul was talking to a caller about prison life in a prison like Maxwell, where I was. I did not have Paul's number on my approved phone list. If I did I may have called his show.

When I first got to prison I tried using the large set of free weights that are on display out in the yard. The prison had many drug dealers from the Miami area and most of them lifted weights during their free time. I saw that one extremely large fellow was between sets with the dumbbells. I walked up and grabbed one of them and began curling. The guy who had just used the weights looked at me disapprovingly and said, "Them is my weights." After this episode, I stuck to walking while listening to the Finebaum show.

I read often. I believe I read 15 books over the three months I was incarcerated. That was a lot for me, since I am not an avid reader, as I have trouble staying put. I read biographies of Pete Rose and Bob Dylan. I also read *Fast-Food Nation*, as I like non-fiction.

Most nights after the evening meal I watched television, read, wrote letters or did my wash. I had to wash every three days or so because of the limited clothes I had. Washing clothes was always time-consuming as there was always a long wait to use the dryers. But, you could pay someone to wash your clothes. Interestingly, the currency at Maxwell Federal Prison was canned mackerel. Inmates actually purchased the cans of mackerel from the "Wal-Mart" and stockpiled them like money. As I recall, the going price to have your clothes washed was "three macks," which was short for cans of mackerel. I am unsure as to why mackerel were adopted as currency. Many of the men did eat them rather than always dine in the camp cafeteria. Money was actually a big no-no. If you wanted to bet on a football game with another inmate it was done with mackerel.

Regarding prison food at Maxwell—it was the absolute worst you could imagine. I learned from reading "Fast Food Nation" that prisoners get the lowest grade of food in the entire food distribution system. I can vouch for that fact. About five of seven days per week the breakfast served consisted of canned peaches and grits. Perhaps once a month we would have eggs but never any meat. Each night of the week a certain type of food would be served. Tuesdays were always chicken and dumplings. The first time I was able to call Phyllis, which was about a week after being processed, I told her how bad the food was. She replied, "Aaron, you are in prison." I never complained to her again about the food, but believe me—it was awful.

Watching TV was a hit or miss. There was a television in the lobby and one in the laundry room, but it was always a group decision as to what was watched. Seldom did my program of choice make the cut. The most popular channel was *Black Entertainment Television*, not the *History Channel*. Sports were pretty popular, which I liked, but this could also be a problem.

One particular Saturday night, LSU, my alma mater, was scheduled to play a football game and I was really looking forward to it all week long. LSU Football is a great escape for any LSU graduate and Tiger fan, and it was especially so for me at the time, given my peculiar circumstance. When I got to the lobby where the TV was located, much to my disappointment the Miami Hurricanes were playing and the drug dealers from Miami would not let me watch LSU, even though I politely asked them if I could. I was crushed.

At the end of the season, which was LSU Head Coach Les Miles' first, the Tigers received a bid to the Peach Bowl in the Atlanta Georgia Dome to play—of all teams—the ninth-ranked Miami Hurricanes. I was elated because I knew I would be able to watch the game, as the Miami guys ruled the TV.

The night before the bowl game, three of the most muscular drug dealers from Miami approached me in the lobby as I was writing a letter. They were physically huge and as they came closer I could not help but notice them. One of them acted as the spokesperson for the group. He said, "Beam! Hand over your shoe laces!" I was scared. I didn't ask for any trouble from them. I replied, "Why?" There was a long pause. The spokesman said, "Because we don't want you to hang yourself when Miami beats LSU's ass tomorrow night!" All three men smiled really big.

When the game began it was only me and thirty big black drug dealers from Miami watching the lone TV in the lobby. From the beginning LSU inflicted a beating on the Hurricanes. The final score was 40-3. Truthfully, the whiping the Tigers gave them was much worse than the score. It was never even a contest. Needless to say, by the end of the game I had the lobby and the TV completely to myself, and I also won ten macks!

The next day I asked one of the Miami inmates if the Hurricanes had a basketball team. He said, "Sure, why do you ask?" I told him, "I'm just checking, because they sure don't have a football team." I thought for a second he was going to punch my card. He replied, "Don't push it, Pops!"

***

The Federal Prison Camp (FPC) at Maxwell is located in Montgomery, Alabama off of Federal Interstates 65 and 85. It is a minimum security prison that houses male offenders from the Middle Alabama Judicial District. At Maxwell there are three buildings that house the inmates. Each sleeps a little over 300. The buildings were named Birmingham, Mobile and Montgomery. Each building was divided into wings that sleep about 50 people. In each wing was a restroom for the entire wing. Inmates slept in bunk beds in open bay areas. There was no privacy, but inmates tried to respect each other's space. It was an unwritten law at Maxwell that you never left your bed without wearing your pants. I discovered this the second night I was there. I went to the restroom wearing only my underwear and tee shirt. On the trip to the toilet I was twice asked "Where the hell are your pants?" One of the guards who conducted regular counts and bed checks was a female.

Inmates for the most part were good about keeping the noise level down. Radios were listened to with headphones, so they were never a problem. However, snoring was a problem. The bunk beds were only a few feet apart and it was amazing how loud some men snored. In an effort to quell the snoring noise, large floor fans were run.

There were about six separate showers with curtains in each bathroom. Inmates respected each other's privacy in the restroom. Most tried to keep themselves covered. I can gladly say that I never saw another inmate completely nude and I never had a problem in the shower.

I was able to make my first phone call after about a week and Phyllis was able to visit me after two weeks. Visiting hours were from 9:00 a.m. until 2:00 p.m. on Saturdays and Sundays and holidays. It was emotional the morning Phyllis dropped me off, but it was even worse when we saw each other during her first visit. There was something about me being in my prison uniform in the visitor's room with the other inmates that made it different, and more difficult. Seeing each other drove home the reality that I was indeed in prison. We were allowed by the guards to embrace each other for a few seconds. We both had tears in our eyes.

The visiting room was a large seating area for about 100 people with large cafeteria style tables. Maxwell visitor's protocol dictated that after the initial welcoming embrace you were not allowed to touch. You could not even hold hands. There were food vending machines along the walls. Phyllis had to put money on a card to be able to make vending machine purchases. The machine food was fabulous compared to the prison cafeteria food, so I looked forward to my vending machine meals on visitation days.

Phyllis and I played a lot of *Scrabble* on visiting days. She usually beat me three out of four times. It was a good visit if I got a machine meal and won at *Scrabble*. At the end of the visit I was always searched before leaving the building. Sometimes it was a complete body search. Visitors are not allowed to bring inmates anything, as they must control contraband flow. During these invasive searches guards looked for cigarettes, money, cell phones, drugs, etc.

Phyllis and Jennifer usually visited on separate days, which allowed me to see someone on most Saturdays and Sundays. The visit lasted the entire visiting time from 9:00 a.m. to 2:00 p.m. However, there was one exception. The weekend LSU played Alabama in football on TV I asked Phyllis to leave early so I could see the kickoff, which is proof that I maintained my priorities while incarcerated.

During visits with my daughter, Jennifer, I was unaware of it, but a few of the inmates were checking her out. A couple of them asked me about her and told me they thought she was pretty. One fellow even asked if he could write to her. With Jennifer's approval I gave him her address. He told Jennifer he was a methamphetamine dealer doing five years—but assured her that he had learned his lesson. He told her he hoped they could meet once he was released. He seemed like a nice fellow, even though he lost a hand in a methamphetamine accident. Jennifer still has his letter he sent her. We often laugh about it and the possibility of them having a relationship, even though she never answered him.

My first phone call to Phyllis was also emotional. Each inmate was allowed a certain amount of call minutes each month, and you of course had to pay for them. The prison system phone rate was not cheap, as you would imagine, as the Wal-Mart and phone centers are real profit centers. During two of the months I used all of my allowed minutes before the month's end. It was difficult not being able to call, as the time on the phone was always the day's high point. When Phyllis answered the phone the first time I was surprised when an automatic recording triggered. It said, "This call is from a Federal prison, if you wish not to accept the call, simply hang up." During this call was when I told her about how bad the food was.

As you might expect, my fellow inmates were a diverse group. I believed the prison was opened with the intent to house only white collar criminals, but over the years non-violent drug dealers had become a large portion of the population housed at Maxwell. If I had to guess I would say that about fifty percent of the inmates there were former dealers. Tax fraud or evasion was probably the most common white collar offense. I met, was introduced to or had pointed out to me lawyers, accountants, bankers, CEO's, CFO's and even one judge, one U.S. Congressman and one doctor.

I got to know the former congressman well. His name was Ed Mezvinsky from Iowa. He was sent to prison for seven years for defrauding investors of more than $10 million. Prosecutors said he collected investors' money during the 1980's for a variety of international business ventures but instead spent the money on a jet-set, globe-trotting lifestyle and failed get-rich-quick schemes. Interestingly, his son, Marc Mezvinsky, is engaged to Chelsea Clinton. Ed worked in the camp library and we got to know each other fairly well. He knew about HealthSouth and talked to me at length about my role in the fraud. He is also writing a book and said that I would be a part of it; which I find funny, because he is in mine.

On a Friday a few days after I arrived, a young bank president from a small Alabama town was assigned to the bunk above mine. He slept nearly around the clock that first weekend. He slept so much that I asked him if he was sick. He said no, that he had partied hard with drugs and alcohol before reporting. He said he wanted to party hard before he did his time—which was several years. I asked why he was in prison and he explained that for years he had been making loans to customers on the condition that he would be paid a kickback for approving the loan. For example, he would allow a customer a $100,000 business loan for a $10,000 fee paid directly to him. He said he was caught because he was living such a high lifestyle that the auditors decided to investigate him. They in turn, discovered the ruse. Strangely, he seemed extremely proud of his criminal past. He was definitely an inmate who I felt upon release might again commit crimes.

I met a different banker from Georgia who made loans that exceeded his loan limits. The loans in question were made to his good friends. He seemed much more remorseful.

When I first arrived to prison I thought I might try to learn about the crimes of each inmate I met. It was natural to wonder each time you met someone. However, I soon learned that it was improper to ask such questions if you had not really gotten to know someone, so I quickly abandoned this plan.

There was an older, bearded man, about my age, who looked like Santa Claus. He looked like the nicest man you might ever meet. One day I told him that I could not imagine why he was in prison. He responded that he had "done a little illegal farming."

Another interesting fellow was a guy who advocated that the Federal Government had no right to collect income taxes. He was famous because he made a living speaking to people on this topic of how to never pay taxes. He reportedly had made an appearance on CBS's *60 Minutes*. Many of the other inmates believed in him and he would occasionally hold classes where he would lecture. I stayed away from him.

The gentleman I self-reported with on November 1 also received only three months. He told me he was guilty of paying cash money to truck drivers who were also drawing unemployment. I believe he was the fall guy for his company. He had grown up in the business and said it was a customary practice, and never realized he might go to prison for it. He was much the country type and lacked a high school diploma. While he was there he studied many long hours and passed his General Education Degree. He was proud of the accomplishment and I was proud of him as well. He was a nice guy who seemed to have gotten himself into something he did not fully understand.

For the most part the drug dealers and the white collar boys kept to themselves. One day I was standing in line for lunch and the two men behind me were comparing ways to make methamphetamine, or "meth," as it is more commonly known. Between them they came up with 22 different methods—no pun intended. They seemed to really enjoy discussing their expertise. Many of these drug dealers were repeat offenders serving their second or third terms at Maxwell.

I became friends with a black drug dealer from Chicago. He moved to South Florida as a young man and worked as a bellboy in a hotel. The job exposed him to drug deals and he started dealing. He came from a poor background and the money was just too easy. He was in the middle of serving his 11th year of a 15-year sentence. We talked often and he said that he was actually afraid of getting out of jail. He said he had become comfortable with prison life. He was active in the prison church and was close to all of the guards. Furthermore, he was somewhat of a supervisor of the men that cleaned the living areas in the Birmingham building. He said he was unsure if he remembered how to drive a car and that from what he saw on television and movies he could tell that the outside world had changed so much he was not sure he could cope. He asked me if he could contact me for help when he was finally released. I said sure, and gave him my home address. I am not sure if I'll ever hear from him, but I would like to help him if I can. He was an extremely nice guy.

In early December Weston Smith reported to the camp. This was a wonderful day for me because Weston and I had always been friends. I was able to show him the ropes the first few days he was there. However, it was awkward since I was going home in about fifty days while he had nearly two years left. I kept thinking how lucky I was to have received only a three-month term. Several of the old-timers used to tell me that they were going to spend more time on the commode than I would in prison.

Weston and I played tennis and Bocee ball often during our off hours. One day Weston and I worked together cleaning the living area. While we cleaned the lavatory we talked about how unfair it was that we were in prison while Richard was still free. We both surmised that Richard would have hated prison life, as it was no fun.

Weston and I both felt that Richard would likely beat the bribery charge. The fact that he won the HealthSouth fraud case, which was a much more difficult one to win, led us to believe that the second trial would end like the first. Other inmates we talked to also felt that Richard would again walk.

The Thanksgiving and Christmas holidays were a hard time for me and Weston. I had to help decorate the Birmingham building. It was depressing. On Christmas Day the warden gave each inmate a bag of candy. I ate it all because it was so much better than the prison food. After the holidays I began to count down the days until my release. I could tell Weston was really down knowing he would still be there for another Christmas.

The day I left, while riding on the bus to the main gate, I saw Weston cutting grass on the Air Force base. I felt bad for him and wondered again if he held a grudge against me for not standing up to Richard.

14

Justice Somewhat Served

"Free at Last, Free at Last!"

On Sunday January 15, 2006, Richard Scrushy stood on the pulpit at the Seventeenth Baptist Church in Anniston, Alabama, with a seated Reverend N.Q. Reynolds on his right, listening intently. According to an *Anniston Star* report, Richard informed the overflowing crowd that he grew up in Selma, Alabama and that in 1965, his father took him to the Pettus Bridge while the turbulent events of the Civil Rights Movement unfolded around them. He explained that his father told him at that time that he wanted him to "see history" so that one day he (Richard) would be able to speak about it and "make change."

On the eve of the Martin Luther King holiday, Richard offered hope to the all-black congregation, reminding them that King's dream was close to being realized. "We're on track to achieve that dream," he said. "The younger generation, they'll only hear about racism."

Although Richard had been acquitted of all related securities fraud charges in June 2005, his legal troubles were far from over. He still faced another Federal trial on bribery charges stemming from two separate $250,000 payments to a Political Action Committee established by Governor Don Siegelman to fund a failed statewide lottery campaign. Moreover, in January 2006 an Alabama circuit court judge ordered Richard to repay more than $52 million in previously paid bonuses and interest as part of a derivatives lawsuit. A similar action in December 2005 cost him $17 million. At this time he also was ordered to pay $1.5

million to settle a HealthSouth employee lawsuit for lost pension investments resulting from the $2.7 billion accounting fraud. Nevertheless, given his success in the first trial, Richard and his army of attorneys were wholly optimistic and even downright cocky as they headed into the second Federal trial.

Donald Watkins, Richard's flamboyant black attorney who once unsuccessfully tried to buy the Minnesota Vikings, mocked the second indictment. "Apparently the spanking we gave them (the Feds) in Birmingham was not sufficient," said Watkins. "We will have to do a better job in Montgomery."

In hindsight, Richard had to be unhappy with Watkins' goading of the Federal Government, because as it turned out, Watkins did not represent Richard in the second trial. Flush with cash earned from the first trial, Watkins instead retired to enjoy the riches of his success. Moreover, Jim Parkman, the "aw-shucks" lawyer who won favor with the Birmingham jury with his "rat and cheese" theatrics, went on to apparently bigger and better dollars by joining the noted Johnnie Cochran Law Firm.

With two of the premier legal eagles of the former Scrushy "Dream Team" gone, it left only Art Leach, a former Federal prosecutor, and an untested cadre of local attorneys, which included the experienced civil rights counsel, Fred Gray. From the onset, Richard's second defense team was at an apparent disadvantage although Leach was a seasoned prosecutor, he simply did not have anywhere near the courtroom experience, charisma or moxie of Watkins or Parkman. The obvious inexperience of the defense team was on display in the courtroom, especially during several heated confrontations with prosecutors. Each of these gaffes adversely affected the defense's case toward the jury.

The prosecutor in the case, Louis Franklin, had a much easier case to try than that of Alice Martin. Juries understand the concept of bribery much easier than the esoteric nature of accounting fraud. Furthermore, there was a paper trail that tied Richard directly to the bribe. Also hurting the defense's case was the fact that the second jury was much more educated than that during the first trial, including a foreman who was an Auburn University fundraiser. Said Franklin, "He knew how fundraising was supposed to work."

In essence, the circumstances surrounding the bribery case were simple, if, that is, you understand politics and the guttural nuances of Alabama campaign finance. Don Siegelman served as Governor of Alabama from 1999 to 2003, after previously serving as Secretary of State, Attorney General and Lieutenant Governor before his 1998 election to the state's top post with 57 percent of the vote. As governor in 1999 Siegelman spearheaded efforts to enact a lottery. In order to do so he formed the political action committee, the Alabama Education Lottery Foundation (AELF), to run ads in favor of the impending statewide referendum. However, after the referendum failed, the ad-related debts far outweighed the funds available in the AELF. This revenue shortfall was a major problem for Siegelman.

At this time Richard Scrushy was a member of the all-important Certificate of Need (CON) Board which exerted great influence on the growth of health care in the State of Alabama. The Certificate of Need Board often decides whether or not a new hospital is built. Since Richard had supported Siegelman's opponent, Bob Riley, in the 1998 gubernatorial election, Siegelman wanted to make sure Richard would pay a premium to retain his all-important position on the CON Board. He demanded Richard pay him $500,000 to keep the seat. Siegelman intended to use this money, along with cash from other sources, to shore up the now deficient AELF.

Because he did not want anyone to know he supported the lottery, Richard arranged for two clandestine payments of $250,000—one from HealthSouth, and another from a company he had ties to, the Maryland-based Integrated Health Services, to AELF.

In 2002 Siegelman appeared to win a narrow re-election under what were considered dubious circumstances. The questionable election returns prompted a late-night vote recount in Baldwin County—a known

Republican stronghold. The 11th-hour re-tabulation swung the election in favor of his opponent, conservative candidate Bob Riley, who won by a margin of less than 3,000 votes among the 1.2 million cast.

By late 2005, when the indictment was handed down, Siegelman had his sights cast firmly on another gubernatorial race. Instead of positive press fueling a promising re-election campaign, he instead faced charges of violating the Racketeer Influenced and Corrupt Organizations Act, known as RICO, along with mail fraud, bribery, extortion and obstruction of justice. Scrushy faced bribery, conspiracy and fraud charges.

When the case went to trial in early May 2006 Siegelman brazenly campaigned for the Democratic nomination on the steps of the Federal Courthouse in Montgomery. However, his efforts proved fruitless. He eventually lost the nomination to Lucy Baxley during the June 6th primary. Siegelman blamed the defeat on the negative fallout from the bribery trial.

The second trial, unlike Richard's first, took only six weeks. Prosecutors described a "pay-to-play" scheme in which campaign donations were necessary to participate in government projects. The prosecution's case hinged on the testimony of former Siegelman aide Nick Bailey, lobbyist Lanny Young and toll bridge developer Jim Allan, whom Scrushy's attorneys creatively labeled "scam artists and liars." The prosecution called only one of five former HealthSouth CFO's to testify against Richard--Mike Martin—who said that Richard bragged to him about the bribe although it was also alleged during the trial that Richard tried to bribe other CON Board members.

In addition to the prosecution's streamlined approach, also hurting Richard's case was the Montgomery venue. In Birmingham, the battle that raged for years between former mayor Richard Arrington and the U.S. Attorney's Office was altogether damaging for the government's case. Montgomery prosecutors were not tainted in this way, allowing for a more open-minded jury.

Undoubtedly the biggest difference between Richard's two trials was how the defense handled the issue of race. During the first trial Donald Watkins avoided racial rhetoric, although he did refer to Richard as "the boy from the other side of the Edmund Pettus Bridge," which was the site of the famous Selma, Alabama clash between local authorities and civil rights activists. In the first trial Richard relied on his use of local television and his high-profile "Amen Corner" in the courtroom.

In stark contrast, Richard's Montgomery defense team's use of race was much more deliberate. While Richard also aired a religious infomercial in Montgomery, it was not as prolonged as the Birmingham version. Moreover, in his closing argument, Richard's counsel, Fred Gray, who had once represented Martin Luther King, Jr., and Rosa Parks, directed the jury to return a not guilty decision "to make Dr. King's dream come true." According to trial reports, as Gray implored the jury, a member of Richard's legal team set up in the background a poster of Martin Luther King's "I Have a Dream" speech. Gray completed his close by loudly raising the intonation of his voice, asking Federal jurors to "fulfill Dr. King's dream and to fulfill that old song…Free at last! Free at last! Thank God almighty we're free at last!"

Gray's semantics proved to be overkill. On June 29, 2006 a jury of seven blacks and five whites returned a guilty verdict in only 11 days, convicting both men of bribery, conspiracy and fraud. Siegelman was also convicted of obstruction of justice, but was acquitted on 25 other counts, including racketeering and extortion.

Adding insult to obvious injury, in August 2006 Richard was ordered by the Alabama Supreme Court to repay $47.8 million in bonuses he wrongly received while the company was actually losing money. The court upheld the earlier circuit court ruling that "without annual net income, Scrushy could not have had the opportunity to earn target bonuses," said Justice Champ Lyons, Jr.

However, Richard's drama continued. In March 2007 Federal prosecutors accused him of trying to flee the country on his 92-foot yacht,

"Chez Soiree." Richard only had permission to travel to South Florida with his family to Disney World. Instead, he left his approved Orlando resort hotel and traveled to Palm Springs where he boarded his yacht and traveled to Miami. Because of this escapade, Richard was subsequently considered a serious flight risk by the courts. Of course, Richard had an excuse. He said his probation officer did not specifically ask him if he was going to Miami. "I can't answer the question until she asks me," said Richard in defense of his actions. U.S. Magistrate Charles Coody told Richard he "was being coy," and reminded him he was a convicted felon. The judge ordered Richard to wear a Global Positioning Satellite (GPS) tracking device, forbade him from going on trips using private travel and required him thereafter to submit detailed itineraries for any future excursions.

In the wake of the judgment, Richard claimed that the HealthSouth donations to the Alabama lottery campaign were the company's "civic duty." He added, "I'm a man who loves God, who loves his country, who loves his family," he told the sentencing judge. "When you go through fire, you turn to God. God is in my life in a major way."

Siegelman commented on his conviction, "If I am truly guilty of this, then every other person in public office had better look out, because everybody is raising money and putting people on boards and commissions." He added, "This is all a right-wing conspiracy!"

On a final note, Richard chimed, "There is no evidence to tie me to these charges. It is sad this could happen in this country."

While prosecutors sought 25 years for Richard and 30 years for Siegelman, neither was sentenced to anywhere near that much time to be served. A full year later, on June 29, 2007, Richard and Siegelman were sentenced for their crimes. Richard, 54, received six years and ten months while Siegelman, 61, received seven years and 4 months. U.S. District Judge Mark Fuller ordered Richard to pay a fine of $150,000 and $1,952.66 per month for incarceration, along with a $267,000 restitution payment which would in turn be donated to the Alabama United Way.

Judge Fuller ordered Siegelman to pay a $50,000 fine and restitution totaling $181,000. Both men, immediately following sentencing, were cuffed and taken away into custody without being able to say goodbye to nearby loved ones—a measure rarely taken with white collar criminals.

15

"Richard's Civil Trial"

"Guilty This Time"

Almost two years after he was sentenced and began his 88-month stay in the Federal Prison at the Beaumont Correctional Complex in Texas, Richard Scrushy returned to Shelby County. However, this wasn't a weekend furlough in Birmingham—it was for Richard to face the next phase the justice system had in store for him—a class-action, civil lawsuit brought against him by disgruntled HealthSouth shareholders. Attorneys representing the jilted lot argued that it was indeed Scrushy who was responsible for the $2.8 billion accounting fraud, despite the contrary findings of the criminal trial jury. "We say it was Scrushy's job to know," plaintiff's attorney John W. Haley stated in his opening remarks.

The civil trial proved to be altogether different from the criminal proceeding. The first trial was rife with courtroom drama, innuendo and semantics. The second trial lacked all of this—and more importantly, a jury, as both sides agreed that it would be best because of publicity, to allow a state court judge, Jefferson County Circuit Court Judge Allwin E. Horn, III, to solely decide the case via bench trial--meaning he and only he would render a decision.

Horn early on in the proceedings issued a gag order to attorneys, preventing the daily press conferences that helped make the first trial a three ring circus. Moreover, most of the rehashed trial evidence was presented to Horn in video depositions rather than with live witnesses, giving the process the entertainment appeal of a syndicated television re-run. Much of the testimony and evidence provided by the plaintiff attorneys dealt with Scrushy's heightened excesses and ridiculous perks enjoyed during his deceptive run as HealthSouth CEO when the company was actually losing money.

The civil trial was also different in that it was the first time Richard Scrushy actually had to take the stand to testify on his own behalf. In the criminal trial Richard never testified, claiming his right to refuse self-incrimination by virtue of the Fifth Amendment to the Constitution. In the civil trial he had no choice.

Once on the stand at the Hugo Black Federal Courthouse Richard claimed that I and not he was the one who hired the CFO's he claimed solely committed the fraud. That of course was a lie. Furthermore, he said that I did not retire, but was instead fired by him. I guess Richard conveniently forgot the press release we ran about my retirement when I walked away from the company back in 1997. Of course, these were small lies compared to the whoppers he continued to tell regarding his supposed lack of knowledge regarding the fraud. Apparently, the judge didn't buy it the second time.

It didn't take long to reach a verdict. On June 18, 2009, only weeks after hearing final arguments from both sides of the case, Judge Allwin E. Horn, III, ruled in favor of the class action plaintiffs—the former HealthSouth shareholders—awarding them a surreal judgment of $2.88 billion against fraudster Richard Marin Scrushy, which amounted to the largest of its kind in American history. Of course, Richard, through his attorney, Susan Walker, forthwith filed an appeal with the Alabama Supreme Court. It is pending.

While some felt that the judgment was as excessive as Richard's former spending habits while he was HealthSouth CEO, many felt it was justified, since no one had a clear picture of how much money he had left. Rumors abounded and still do today that Richard stashed money in the Bahamas by starting a bank with Donald Watkins, and that he has millions in untouchable overseas investments and holdings. However, in 2005, when the government unsuccessfully tried him on securities fraud, his net worth was conservatively estimated at $300 million.

Richard has, of course, returned to his Beaumont home and the *Birmingham News* has reported that his wife Leslie has vacated the Vestavia Hills home and moved their kids to Beaumont to be near Richard. The legal process of seizing Richard's many assets is underway. Already there is disagreement among the lawyers as to how the spoils should be distributed. The big question is how much should be left to Richard and his family, how much should the lawyers get, how much should HealthSouth the corporation get, and finally, how much the suing shareholders should receive. All I can think of is, "What a free-for-all!"

It is crystal clear that no matter how much is ultimately taken from Richard's remaining recoverable assets, there will not be enough to go around and make all affected parties happy. Everyone would be much better off today if Richard had been paid $1 billion to just go away in 1996.

Epilogue

The wagon ride is over. What a trip it was. It is difficult to summarize such a complex, twisting story. However, if I had to distill it to a word, I would say "tragedy." Why did we let it happen? This is the biggest question. While I feel the book does a good job of telling the story of HealthSouth, it certainly still leaves one wondering "why" it happened. Was it because Richard exhibited the tendencies of a greedy sociopath? Was it because of me not having the moral bearing to stop him? Or, is it today's society and its changing values that have brought the entire world economy to its proverbial knees?

In 1806 Webster's Dictionary defined success as "being generous, prosperous, healthy and kind." Today, Webster's defines success as "the attainment of wealth, fame and rank." One can certainly see how attitudes and beliefs have changed across the world in just two hundred years. These changes have ostensibly altered the way business ethics is viewed and practiced. Moreover, these changes have had disastrous effects, with HealthSouth obviously being one of the prime examples.

I do believe an utter lack of business ethics has played a huge role in corporate fraud. I did not discuss it much, but "Wall Street pressures" were omnipresent. Wall Street fueled Richard's zeal and ambition. Many of the insider dealings that Richard took part in were suggested by venture capitalists and investment bankers. Richard cut many deals because "The Street" was saying, "It is okay—you can do it because everyone else is." Furthermore, the stock analysts wrote what we wanted them to write and we told them what the bankers said would keep the stock trading high.

I was recently interviewed by the President of the Association of Certified Fraud Examiners in preparation for my speaking engagement at their 2009 National Meeting. They gave me two interesting books to read. One is titled, *Snakes in Suits: When Psychopaths go to Work*, by Paul Babiak and Robert D. Hare and the other, *Frankensteins of Fraud*, by

Joseph T. Wells. I found both books riveting and each helped me understand why the HealthSouth fraud occurred.

According to behavioral scientist Robert Merton in the aforementioned title, *Frankensteins of Fraud*, much of the crimes that occur in the United States of America come from "our overwhelming emphasis on money and the fact that there are barriers that cannot be surmounted by most people to obtain the kind of money they'd like to possess." Merton says that most of us settle for what we can get, and seek and find happiness within that normal paradigm. However, he says that there are always going to be others that will "feel compelled to make their fortune by stomping on others and living lives that they know might at any moment end in disaster..."

I would like to examine two of the more prominent monsters mentioned in the book *Frankensteins of Fraud*—Charles Ponzi and "Crazy" Eddie Antar. Many older Americans know these notorious names and have heard of the horror stories related to their committed frauds. In both of these cases it seems that these "Frankensteins" were powerless to overcome the visceral forces from within themselves to do the right thing. As a result, many good people have fallen victim to their apparently innate imperfections.

Charles Ponzi was destined to be a criminal miscreant. By the time he was 21 he was no longer wanted in his homeland of Italy, having been repeatedly arrested for gambling, thievery and forgery. According to those that knew him during his early years, Ponzi never sought legitimate work, yet still talked about one day having the finer things in life.

Ponzi's scheme, of which so many subsequent ruses have been labeled, was as simple as it was devastating. Emerging before government regulation during a time when individual investing was just coming of age, Ponzi offered victims an opportunity to earn two dollars for every one dollar invested by buying postal coupons in Italy. Of course, Ponzi absconded millions of investor dollars intended for postal coupons to pay old debts and to fuel his lavish lifestyle. By preying on the ignorance and confidence of others, Ponzi's scheme worked to perfection, until his greed surpassed his ability to pay debts and his former clients. Ultimately, his house of cards predictably crashed and he was exposed as a fraud, convicted and jailed. Subsequently, all of Ponzi's attempts toward legitimacy were doomed. He failed as a publisher, a land shark, a business manager of an airline, a landlord and even a lowly hotdog salesman—just as he had in the beginning as a crook.

Eddie Antar of Brooklyn, New York was born into a family of criminal enterprisers. His father, Sam, taught Eddie and the other family members how to ply their fraudulent trade of purposely non-reporting cash sales. With the Antars, cheating on their books was not just a way to save on paying taxes—it was a way of life. Eddie began a chain of discount electronic stores—"Crazy Eddie's," before there were the large chains like *Best Buy* and *Circuit City*. The model was obviously strong, but the company's business and accounting practices lacked a certain critical ingredient--ethics. Crazy Eddie and his family not only cheated their customers and taxing authorities, they wanted to cheat investors—which is where the real money was. By gradually reducing their regular skimming practices, Crazy Eddie's family was able to make their stores appear more profitable than they really were; which enabled them to eventually become a publicly traded company. Predictably, assets and profits were subsequently overstated, allowing for his family to "earn" $80 million as a result of the massive retail fraud gone public. Like Ponzi, Eddie was eventually discovered to be a fraud through the undeniable forces of capitalism; and like Ponzi, was tried and jailed, albeit after an unsuccessful flight to Israel.

One can see the inherent similarities Richard Scrushy has with these famous fraudsters. The authors of *Snakes in Suits* give an in-depth, clinical look into the personalities of those that commit corporate fraud. Like *Frankensteins of Fraud*, I highly recommend it as a means to understand the HealthSouth fraud.

I feel that there is another reason as to why or how the HealthSouth fraud happened. I call it the "bubble cycle." I am old enough now that I have studied or actually seen periods in our economy when a bubble develops and one day finally bursts. The stock market crash of 1929 was caused by a bubble in stock prices. Everyone was getting rich and hot money was chasing stocks higher and higher.

I lived in Houston, Texas during the 1970's when real estate prices went crazy. I bought a home in the early 1970's for $28,000 and sold it just a few years later for $75,000. It seemed like everyone was in a land speculation deal, if not four or five. It was all done with borrowed money and you paid your loan off once you flipped the land to another speculator. When this bubble burst I could hardly believe the results. Many ordinary people lost thousands of dollars they really did not have, and Texas Commerce Bank failed. Prior to its failure I always thought of it as the safest bank in the nation.

Most recently we have all seen the real estate market (along with the economy) collapse because of the sub-prime mortgage debacle. HealthSouth, Richard Scrushy, myself, and many others were in the middle of an "alternative healthcare Stock Market Bubble." It was a bubble that we played a great part in starting. By the early 1990's the hot money was chasing stocks like HealthSouth and charlatans like Richard Scrushy. This allowed Richard to start or be associated with many of the bubble companies that developed. Companies like MedPartners and Capstone Capital were really bad economic models but they were taken up by the fast rising economic tide.

These bubble cycles are great breeding grounds for corporate fraud, because these people who place money and material possessions ahead of all other things can eventually run out of control.

Now for the big question: What would have happened if Bill Owens and I had said no to Richard on that summer day in 1996? I have been asked this many times. The short answer is that everyone, with maybe the exceptions of lawyers and forensic accountants, would be much better off today. That is why what happened is so tragic. The amount of fraudulent recordings in the HealthSouth books was somewhere around $2.5 billion.

These were just paper entries. Two and a half billion in actual dollars were not taken out of the company. However, hard dollars have been paid by HealthSouth because of the fraud. From 2003-2005 professional fees associated with the reconstruction of HealthSouth's financial records totaled $447 million. In December 2004 the company agreed to pay the United States Government $325 million because of the fraud and in June 2005 the company agreed to pay the $100 million to settle claims brought by the Securities and Exchange Commission (SEC). Moreover, in 2009 the investment banking groups UBS and Ernst & Young each agreed to pay $100 million without admitting fault to the HealthSouth fraud.

I cannot even start to guess how much has been spent on lawyers for all involved with the fraud, but it is surely into the hundreds of millions. In total, everyone would have been much better off if the company had agreed in 1996 to pay Richard Scrushy $1 billion for him to go away. However, would Richard have taken the deal?

In retrospect, I can remember early on when HealthSouth and Richard's many other companies were riding the crest of the health care bubble. At this time, Richard's personal fortune was worth well over six or seven hundred million dollars. I recall one day in Richard's office I asked him if he ever thought of selling the company—of getting out—cashing in completely. He replied, "Not yet—one day we'll all go fishing," he said, "but not just yet."

Back to the question: What if Bill Owens and I had said, "No?" Besides saving all of these hard dollars we have discussed, those involved in the fraud would not be felons. Families have been broken apart and many loved ones emotionally damaged because of the fraud. This of course could have been prevented. If we had reported true earnings that day the stock would have certainly taken a hit.

While we are making assumptions let us assume Richard would have gotten his ego under control and began placing his full attention on the company. Many millions could have been saved. In my opinion the stock would have recovered and Wall Street would not have been questioning the legitimacy of our numbers like they did before the fraud was discovered. Exactly where the stock would have traded I cannot say, but it would never have gone into the pennies as it did in 2003, when stockholders lost billions. Because the quality of the HealthSouth-provided health care has always been good, the stock has recovered much of its value and the company has been reinstated on the New York Stock Exchange. It is easy to speculate that the stock would be even higher today if it had not gone through so much tumult resulting from the fraud.

***

There are undoubtedly hundreds, possibly even thousands of Richard Scrushy stories out there. If Richard was anything, he was consistently bad in the way he treated people. It was simply the tact he chose to get what he wanted. He was reckless in his pursuit of success. Moreover, he was equally reckless when he punished those who criticized or made fun of him; which leads me to a final Richard story.

In 1997, HealthSouth sponsored the popular celebrity spring golf classic at Greystone Country Club. The tournament, which offered valuable prizes and awards to the victors, was dubbed, "The HealthSouth Pro-Am." According to Paul Finebaum, it was the year that he, Florida Head Coach Steve Spurrier, Randy Owen vocalist of the world-famous music group *Alabama*, and Richard Scrushy played together in a foursome.

According to Paul, the foursome was on the tee box to the par three seventh hole where two or three thousand spectators had gathered to get a glimpse of the celebrity match play. Richard teed his ball and addressed it. He made a full swing and badly whiffed--flubbing the ball only a few feet where it rested at the front edge of the tee box. Amidst a few groans from the crowd Richard audaciously walked to his ball, picked it up and returned it to the tee where he quickly re-addressed it and lofted it unimpressively toward the green.

Coach Spurrier was incredulous. He immediately looked at Paul and whispered, "He just cheated!" Paul, knowing Richard's personality and nature, tried to downplay the shifty move by simply nodding his head, and by whispering to Coach Spurrier to "calm down." However, Paul noticed that Randy overheard Spurrier's objection.

Two holes later, on the ninth, Richard again addressed his ball. His shot sliced badly to the right of the fairway, sailed over the tennis court fence and bounced once safely over the net onto the clay court. Like clockwork, Spurrier chimed, "Fifteen-Love." As would be expected, the jibe was met with much laughter from everyone, except Richard, of course.

A couple of weeks later Paul ran into Richard's sidekick, referred to earlier as Pal #1, and was informed by him that Steve Spurrier was "finished." Paul asked him what he meant. Pal #1 explained that Randy Owen had explained to Richard that Spurrier had accused him of cheating and that the objection, along with the good-natured ribbing two holes later had sent Richard fuming. Since HealthSouth sponsored the event, Richard decided not to invite Spurrier to any future HealthSouth Pro-Ams. Needless to say, I'm sure Steve was crushed.

Eight years after the incident, in 2005, the year that the HealthSouth fraud trial began, Spurrier returned to Greystone for the celebrity classic that was obviously no longer sponsored by HealthSouth. Paul again was grouped into Spurrier's foursome. When they approached the seventh tee it rekindled the duo's memory of Richard. Paul mentioned to Spurrier that Richard was under indictment for fraud, which prompted Spurrier to comment, "Scrushy…I knew he was a cheater back then."

Afterword

It is August 2009 and it has been 13 years since I first took part in the HealthSouth fraud. Over six years have passed since the spring day in 2003 when I heard the troubling words, "Breaking news from Birmingham, Alabama" on my television. Of course, not a day goes by that I do not think about what a mess I made of my life. However, not all is terrible.

Phyllis works for a social services agency. Jennifer has a great job as an events manager at the Grand Hotel in Point Clear, Alabama, and my lawn care business, "Green Beam Lawn Service," is hard, but honest work. Furthermore, with the economy in the shape it is in, the three of us are lucky to have good jobs.

Late in 2007 I called the Dean of the School of Business at LSU to see if they would consider having me speak to their business students. I think he was a little surprised by the call and he said he needed to think about it. However, within a week he called back and said the school would like to have me as a guest speaker, and that they were actually excited about the idea. My talk was eventually given to several combined classes of MBA's and senior accounting students. I simply told the story of how I met Richard, started HealthSouth, the success HealthSouth became, and of course how it all went so catastrophically wrong. The speech was simply a greatly-condensed version of the book you just read.

The initial speech was well-received and I have been invited back to LSU nearly a dozen times in the past two years; and last year Auburn University called me and asked if I would speak to their students. I did and several Auburn accounting professors encouraged me to engage other universities about speaking to their students. By now the sub-prime mortgage debacle was taking its deadly toll on the national economy, Bernie Madoff had become a household name and business schools across the country were quickly realizing that the lack of business ethics in the business world is a real problem. I took the Auburn professors' advice and began to proactively contact schools about having me speak to them.

A friend designed an Internet website to help market my speaking services and soon I was receiving regular inquiries about my speech on business ethics. To date I have visited or I am scheduled to visit over 20 different universities. Furthermore, I have also spoken to corporations and various related business associations. As a speaker I am somewhat of a rare commodity because the CFO's of Enron, Worldcom and Tyco are still incarcerated and will be for years to come.

I truly believe that speaking to students and other business people is important. I always try to explain how you can become involved in a fraud when you never thought you would. When you work for a company that stresses profits at all costs it is a potentially destructive situation. I explain that you must seriously consider the company's values when taking a job, and above all else--be prepared to walk away from an otherwise good job if you are asked to commit or be a party to fraud.

Business schools are trying to teach ethics. Some might argue that a person is either ethical or unethical, regardless of education. I do not think it is that black or white. Learning is a process and repetition is part of it. I believe ethics training is much like the training the heroic pilot, Captain Chesley "Sully" Sullenberger, who saved the passengers on the flight that plunged into the Hudson River, received. Sully was trained his entire life to handle the dire situation, and when it finally happened, he was able to make the decisions that allowed him and many others in his care to live. When the critical time came, his instincts took over, and he and his passengers survived. If today's future business executives are similarly trained in high school, college, graduate school and on the job about ethical behavior, it will become instinctive. This type of training has not been part of our past American business culture.

Speaking to college students has greatly helped me deal with the shame and pain I feel because of my actions and inactions while I was CFO at

HealthSouth. I have received many emails and letters from those I've addressed and they tell me what I am doing is worthwhile. This helps.

I do ask for a fee when I speak. I do not always receive one, however. Many schools and business associations have a policy that they do not pay felons. I understand that. Moreover, because of the current economy many schools simply do not have the money to pay speakers. Many times I have waived the fee and spoken anyway.

The money I do make from speaking is not much, but every bit helps. Phyllis and I would like to retire again someday. I am sure there are people who believe I still am wealthy, but this is simply not true. Trust me—if you can—I would not be mowing lawns in the South Alabama summer heat if it was not necessary.

As I complete this project I realize that I could continue to write about this story, as it is still developing daily in the regional and national news. As of press time Karon Brooks-Harris, Richard's second wife, is writing her own book about her life with Richard and the abuse she endured living with him. I look forward to reading it, as I am certain it will help answer many more questions.

I realize that Richard Scrushy in all probability will sue me when this book is published. So be it. I let Richard ruin my life by not standing up to him when it was my job to do so. This book is the truth and I am not going to let the fear of him suing me stop me from finally telling the truth. The time has come, Richard. The truth is that I should have stood up to you a long time ago.

The End...for now.

References

"Accountant Describes How HealthSouth Fraud Happened." *USA Today*. January 28, 2005. http://www.usatoday.com/money/industries/health/2005-01-28-scrushy_x.htm

Babiak, Paul & Hare, Robert D. Snakes In Suits: When Psychopaths Go To Work. Harper Collins, 2007. New York, New York.

Carnns, Ann. "HealthSouth Ex-Finance Chief Gets Three-Month Prison Term." *The Wall Street Journal*. August 26, 2005.

Carlton, Bob. "Disgraced HealthSouth Co-Founder Seeks his Redemption in the Soil." *Birmingham News*, July 16, 2006, Vol. 19, Issue 125, 1A.

Carlton, Bob. "Field of Beam's." *The Birmingham News*. December 27, 2000.

Cohen, Adam. "The Strange Case of an Imprisoned Alabama Governor." *The New York Times*. September 10, 2007.

Crawford, Krysten. "Ex-HealthSouth CEO Scrushy Walks." *CNNMoney.com*. June 28, 2005. http://money.cnn.com/2005/06/28/news/newsmakers/scrush_outcome/index/htm

Farrell, Greg. "Against the Odds, Scrushy Walks out of Court Free Man." *USA Today*. June 28, 2005.

Farrell, Greg. "Bright Ideas Gone Bust Can Lead to Corporate Fraud." *USA Today*. August 1, 2006.

Farrell, Greg. "Former HealthSouth CEO Scrushy Turns Televangelist." *USA Today*. October, 25, 2004.

Farrell, Greg. "From Emperor to Outcast." *USA Today*. May 29, 2003.

Farrell, Greg. "Scrushy Guilty of Bribery Case Involving Ex-Governor." *USA Today*. June 30, 2006.

Finebaum, Paul. Personal Interview. Birmingham, Alabama. April 14, 2009.

Gullo, Karen. "Brocade Legal Bills Outpace Profits in Options Cases (Update 3)." February 9, 2009. *Bloomberg.com*.

Grow, Brian. "Richard Scrushy's 'Amen Corner.'" *BusinessWeek*. January 20, 2006.

Hallman, Ben. "A Tale of Two Trials: Lesson Learned From the Scrushy Story." *American Lawyer*. February 15, 2007.

HealthSouth Annual Report, 2005.

HealthSouth Timeline – Part I (1983-1988). March 20, 2005. www.scrushyreport.com/wordpress/index.php?p=72

"HealthSouth Pays Nearly $8 Million for Overcharging U.S. Health Care Programs." May 22, 2001. www.usdoj.gov/opa/pr/2001/May/228civ.htm

Helyar, John. "The Man Who Saved Richard Scrushy." July 11, 2005. *Fortune.com*.

Helyar, John. "The Insatiable King Richard." *CNNMoney.com/Fortune*. July 7, 2003. http://money.cnn.com/magazines/fortune/fortune_archive/2003/07/07/345534/index.htm

Hubbard, Russell. "Daniel Corporation to Buy HealthSouth Headquarters." *Birmingham News*. December 12, 2007.

Hubbard, Russell. "HealthSouth Co-Founder to Admit to Bank Fraud."
The Birmingham News. April 25, 2003.

Hubbard, Russell. "Judge: Richard Scrushy is Responsible for
HealthSouth Fraud." *Birmingham News*, June 18, 2009.

Hubbard, Russell & Walton, Val. "Scrushy Testifies on HealthSouth
Tenure 'From Beginning to End." *The Birmingham News.* June
17, 2008.

Johnson, Bob. "Ex-HealthSouth Chief "Flight Risk." *The Baton Rouge
Advocate.* March 31, 2007, 6D.

Johnson, Carrie. "Five Years for HealthSouth Fraud." *The Washington
Post.* December 10, 2005.

Johnson, Carrie. "Richard Scrushy's Chief Believer." *The Washington
Post.* May 18, 2006.

Kinsley, Michael. "The Lord and Richard Scrushy." *The Washington
Post.* July 3, 2005.

Morse, Dan, Terhune, Chad & Carrns, Ann. "Clean Sweep—
HealthSouth's Scrushy Is Acquitted." *The Wall Street Journal.*
June 29, 2005.

Reeves, Jay. "I Should Have Stood Up to Richard Scrushy." *The
Washington Post.* August 26, 2005.

Roberts, Joel. "Ex-HealthSouth CEO Acquitted."
http://www.cbsnews.com/stories/2005/06/28/business/main704807
.shtml. June 28, 2005.

Rodengen, Jeffrey L. The Story of HealthSouth. Write Stuff Enterprises,
Inc., Fort Lauderdale, Florida, 2002.

Romero, Simon. "Will the Real Richard Scrushy Please Step Forward; Race, Religion and the HealthSouth Founder's Trial. *The New York Times.* February 17, 2005.

Smith, Weston. Telephone Interview. April 12, 2009.

Stuart, Alix. "Keeping Secrets: How Five CFO's Cooked the Books at HealthSouth." *CFO Magazine.* June, 2005. http://www.cfo.com/article.cfm/4007474

Taub, Stephen. "Former HealthSouth CFO Gets Three Years." *CFO Magazine.* September 12, 2006.

Thomas, Bill. "Scrushy's Properties." *The Birmingham News.* April 6, 2003.

Tomberlin, Michael. "Ex-CFO Sentenced to Prison and Fined." *The Birmingham News.* August 26, 2005.

Tomberlin, Michael. "HealthSouth Probe Nets Two More Pleas." *The Birmingham News.* April 1, 2003.

Tomberlin, Michael & Walton, Val. "Execs Plotted to Take Firm Private, Witness Says." *The Birmingham News.* April 25, 2003.

Walton, Val. "Fifth CFO Pleads Guilty: Beam Admits Band Fraud for HealthSouth, Links Scrushy." *The Birmingham News.* May 6, 2003.

Walton, Val & Tomberlin, Michael. "Scrushy's Ex-Guard Blames Owens." *The Birmingham News.* April 16, 2003.

Warren, Brandy. "Scrushy Speaks at Southern Christian Leadership Conference Program." *The Anniston Star.* January 16, 2006.

Wells, Joseph T. Frankensteins of Fraud. Obsidian Publishing, 2000. Austin, Texas.

Whitmire, Kyle. "Openers: Suits: Did Anyone Ask About a Yacht?" *The New York Times*. April 15, 2007.

Whitmire, Kyle. "Scrushy Watch: The Weston Smith Juncture." April 6, 2006, Volume IX, Issue 32.
    Birminghamweekly.com/archived/pages/2005031_scrushy.php

If you enjoyed "The Wagon to Disaster" by Aaron Beam, with Chris Warner, you may enjoy:

"Professional Bone"

A Novel

By Chris Warner

Ron Barton is everybody's All-American. A former small-town hero turned Southern collegiate baseball star and Rhodes Scholar, he is the atypical high-profile physician. Barton's expertise in orthopedics takes him to the Deep South's medical Mecca of Birmingham, Alabama, where he excels in the operating room as quickly as he did on the red clay diamonds for Auburn University.

Philip Lucci is a rising star in the lucrative field of rehabilitative sports medicine. A former gas station attendant and brick mason turned physical therapist/entrepreneur; he is as much of an anomaly as Dr. Barton. Lucci's laser-like vision to create the *McDonald's* of worldwide rehabilitative care and sports medicine is as powerful as his insatiable drive for wealth, fame and social rank. Like Barton, he too is a product of the Deep South; but the similarities end there. Lucci is the archetype Machiavellian dictator bent on success. Barton is the consummate professional seeking self-actualization through innovation and heightened care. Unbeknownst, they are on a collision course that will rock Birmingham, rehabilitative medicine and ultimately, Wall Street, to their collective cores.

The consummate manipulator, Lucci makes a living off of the knowledge and weakness of others. Operating like a benevolent Mafia Don, he is as brutal as he is cunning. A star as bright as Barton's cannot go unnoticed by Lucci's all-discerning focus. Lucci makes him an offer he seemingly cannot refuse—to be a part of his budding rehabilitative health care empire—at more than double his current salary in an office that is as ostentatious as his potential benefactor. But refuse Barton does, as he is not in the least bit impressed by money, or Lucci's phony veneer. Unaccustomed to rebuke, Lucci is incensed by Barton; and as a result, he endeavors to ruin him—as fitting payback.

Amanda Lucci, Philip's second wife, is a former Miss Alabama and cheerleader for the Alabama Crimson Tide. Nine years the junior of her husband, Philip, a deprived youth fueled her misguided worldview; until she matured and saw the tragedy of her life. Bored with the Earthly comforts lavished upon her by her overbearing, compromised husband, she retreats increasingly to the high-end escape world of polo, where she meets and falls in love with Dr. Ron Barton, whom she hopelessly admires for his rugged looks and purposeful existence.

Lucci's bodyguards and surveillance team soon learn of the affair and inform their boss. It is just the edge he needs to ruin his recalcitrant detractor. Having already grown tired of Amanda's continued rebuffs, Lucci now has the perfect vengeance plan firmly in place.

In the aftermath of the set-up, Lucci's company rises as quickly as Barton's disgraceful fall. Although Ron and Amanda ultimately marry after a nasty, highly-scandalized and extremely public divorce, his practice suffers. In the meantime, Lucci becomes a darling of Wall Street and remarries yet another, even younger Miss Alabama and former television talk show host, Clara Roberts, whose vast contacts in the media world become the Fountainhead for Lucci's far-reaching health care dynasty.

While Barton is weakened, he is not defeated. He vows revenge. Working through his trusted colleagues he learns of a chink in Lucci's apparently impregnable armor. Barton discovers that as Lucci's success grew, so did his competitors, inevitably shrinking an already competitive patient pool. To maintain Wall Street's continued expectations, Lucci has resorted to forcing his accounting sycophants to brazenly cook the books by creating thousands of false revenue entries totaling in the billions of dollars.

Barton devises his own plan to leak this information to the FBI and raze Lucci's precariously shaky house of cards. But Lucci's resourcefulness proves to be perplexing, as his intelligence officers learn of the "rats" that threaten their excessive existence; which in turn, reset Lucci's unforgiving sights. Barton again finds himself in the crosshairs— and he is not alone, as his faithful colleagues are now in danger of succumbing to Lucci's growing, fear-fueled malice.

As the plot unfolds, it takes the reader on a tortuous, unforgettable courtroom ride. Lucci, the reinvented televangelist catering to a majority black congregation, is first found innocent of securities fraud as a result of shameless jury pool tainting. However, he is subsequently convicted of a Federal bribery charge involving a clandestine payoff to the sitting Alabama Governor to maintain his powerful position on the Certificate of Need (CON) Board that controls the growth and direction of health care in the state. In the end, Lucci lands predictably in Federal prison; but his long-time dream of building a world-class digital, rehabilitative hospital continues nevertheless, albeit with the tweaking of its new standard-bearer, Dr. Barton--who puts his own innovative stamp on its construction and subsequent administration.

Professional Bone is a fast-paced, romantic action thriller that seeks to draw semblance to the ongoing, negative impacts that corporate greed, fraud and indifferent citizenship have had on American free market capitalism.

Available at respected book sellers.